A GOOD WORK

JACKIE JENKINS

"

"But when Jesus was aware of it, He said to them, 'Why do you trouble the woman? For she has done a good work for Me.'"

– Matthew 26:10 (NKJV)

DEDICATION

To the Lord my God, there is none like You. There are no limits to You—no heights nor depths. And yet somehow, You are mindful of me. Thank You for showing me what greatness truly is. It is Your greatness that has surrounded, taught, and sustained me. Just as it is Your greatness that sustains the heavens and earth.

"Great is the Lord, and greatly to be praised; and His greatness is unsearchable."

– Psalm 145:3

To my parents, thank you for always being there.

TABLE OF CONTENTS

PART 2: Positive, Thought-Provoking Discussions

INTRODUCTION

A Good Work is based on Matthew 26:1-13. While writing this book, I was reminded of some of the reasons woman was created. God made woman first to reflect Himself. I believe this is one of the reasons why He referred to her as a "helper." His Holy Spirit, that is the Spirit of God, is the Helper (John 15:26). Being made in His image, we are to reflect His love, His compassion, His faithfulness, and so on. Second, we are to be helpers to mankind and to ourselves. And third, we are to be fruitful, multiply, and rule over everything on the earth (Gen. 1:27-2:20). As women, we were designed as part of God's divine plan. And in this book, we will see how God utilized a woman who, unbeknownst to her, did a good work for His Kingdom.

This woman was in Bethany, a town just outside of Jerusalem. The scenario surrounding her might suggest that this was set up for anyone other than a woman. Jesus and His disciples were on their way to Jerusalem after He had spent the day teaching them through parables. While on their way, Jesus reminded His disciples of what was going to take place within a few days. However, there is no indication that His disciples were even mindful of what He was saying or what it truly meant. The Passover was two days away; Jesus would be betrayed and, shortly thereafter, crucified. How could His disciples not respond to the weight of this information? The truth of it had already determined their destiny. But as it appears, there was no acknowledgment that they even knew what He was talking about.

Jesus and His disciples continued their journey, stopping in the town of Bethany. They went to the house of Simon the Leper (Matt. 26:6). A woman with a bottle of very expensive oil entered the house and began to pour the oil onto Jesus' head. His disciples became angry over what they perceived to be a waste of valuable goods. Jesus defended the woman's actions and began questioning His disciples' motives. What did they have to do with what was taking place between Him and the woman in Bethany? The time they should have asked questions was when Jesus informed them that He would be betrayed and crucified. No one had anything to say until just then. How can that even make sense? After all, she owned the oil and could do whatever she wanted with it.

His disciples appeared to back off once Jesus began to defend the woman in Bethany, for this was not His first-time defending women. He gave His approval of Mary when she sat at His feet and would not leave Him—even when her sister, Martha, requested help (Luke 10:42). Jesus also defended the woman who wiped His feet with her tears and dried them with her hair (Luke 7:38). It was clear that the woman in Bethany had His approval regardless of the cost of this perfumed oil, so perhaps this gave His disciples a sense of how He felt about what she was doing. Things were different with the woman in Bethany. She performed a task that not only had purpose but also had an expected, sustainable end. This was so, even if she did not know it.

Jesus' disciples were very upset. They wanted to know the purpose of Jesus getting such special treatment. What would be the result of pouring the expensive oil on His head? There had to be a good reason, but they were clueless. Why would Jesus teach them Kingdom lessons and not share what was going on with the costly activity they were witnessing? This obviously made no sense to them.

Jesus, of course, did not give in to His disciples' demands for an explanation about the use of such an expensive perfumed oil. Instead, He explained what appeared to satisfy them at least for the moment. Only God the Father, the Son, and the Holy Spirit knew what was really taking place. Although it seemed Jesus was unable to get His disciples' full attention earlier when He mentioned His impending crucifixion, He finally had it—all because of what the woman in Bethany did.

Did this woman make her way through town with an expensive bottle of perfumed oil just to pour it on Jesus' head? What was the meaning of this action? What was this good work Jesus mentioned? His disciples were the first who wanted to know.

Today, God still has work for us to do. Though there are many who think women should not be in ministry, we should thank God that His thoughts are higher than our thoughts and that our ways are not His ways (Isa. 55:8-9). God is in control. He does not only place us into ministry, but He places the ministry into us. Therefore, no one can take the ministry away from us. All glory be to God!

As for the woman in Bethany, did she succeed at completing her assignment? Or did she fail? Well, the woman did not fail. Jesus made it clear that she successfully completed her task. He said to His disciples, "'... For she has done a good work for Me'" (Matt. 26:10).

Ways to Use This Book

The first chapter gives an overview of how woman, along with man, fell from Gods' gift of paradise and into this place called the world. The next three chapters give insight into the characteristics of those in the scriptures of Matthew 26:1-5. Chapter 5 begins to focus on the woman in Bethany, and the good work she performed.

This book is meant to inform and encourage you. Pray and ask God to give you understanding as you read. Be receptive, mindful, and patient in discovering that while some things might seem familiar even in your own life, you do not have to feel judged. Instead, feel challenged to become all that God has designed you to be. As I wrote this book, there were things that I could identify with. At times, it seemed the enemy wanted me to regret mistakes I had made in the past and resent God for pointing them out. But I chose to see things through the eyes of God. It made me want to change areas of my own life. That is a good thing—a positive thing.

Some words shared may hurt, but sometimes wounds heal quicker if the bandage is pulled off. Read this book wanting more of God, more of His grace, and more of His goodness. He wants these things for you. There is no condemnation with God, but He will convict through His Holy Spirit because that is His love toward us. Yes, the Lord loves you, and He wants the best for you. And that is to live freely in His presence. You were not created just for God's purposes but also for His glory.

Discussions can be done in groups for support, or they can be done in private for deeper personal reflection.

Note: References to God, Jesus, and the Holy Spirit are in persons of He, Him, His, They, One, and are capitalized.

CHAPTER ONE

UNDER DEVELOPMENT

Based on the behavior displayed by men and women today, one can say humans are still under development. This, of course, is not God's fault. He completed His work in six days, and on the seventh day He rested (Gen. 1:31-2:3). In Genesis 2, the Bible says the heavens and the earth and all the host of them were finished. This does not include mankind. Yes, man had already been made by God and was "good," but there was no mention of man being "finished." While the heavens and the earth played host to the moon, stars, sun, rain, plants, and animals, man was made in the image of God. Mankind was given dominion over the earth, which means he was given authority and the right to rule over everything on the earth. You remain the host when someone comes into your home. They don't rule your home. You rule because it's your right to rule. It's your home. God rules in heaven, above the heavens, on the earth, and beneath the earth, yet He gave man authority over everything on the earth.

Being made in the image of God gives humans an advantage that no other creation has. While Adam and Eve both fell short of the glory God bestowed upon them, this book will focus more on the role of women. Because of Eve's sin, one might think God condemned women to never rise up again. When God asked Eve what she had done, she replied, "The serpent deceived me, and I ate" (Gen. 3:13). And because of this, God placed woman in a position where love would be painful for her physically and emotionally. The birth of the children she would one day carry would bring forth physical pain, and her husband, the man she loved, would bring forth heartache and emotional pain (v.16). In short, it seemed woman had been positioned so that her life would be surrounded by pain.

Before God punished Adam and Eve, they were in a good place. They were different from the other creatures God made because they were created in His image. Although they were covered in flesh, they operated as spiritual beings. Because they saw themselves as spiritual beings, they did not recognize their naked flesh as anything unnatural. Adam and Eve could walk around the garden naked and commune with God face to face, unlike humans today. It wasn't until they ate from the Tree of Knowledge of Good and Evil that their eyes were opened; they realized they were naked (Gen. 3:7). They had transitioned from a spiritual position to the knowledge of a worldly position. Eating from the forbidden tree was the act of sin that prevented man from developing and maintaining eternal life in the presence of God (vv 17-19).

As God began to question Adam regarding what he and Eve had done, Adam immediately abandoned Eve. This was before God even announced her fate to experience pain in life. Adam answered God saying, "... 'The woman whom You [emphasis added] gave *to be* with me, she gave me of the tree, and I ate'" (v. 12). This was a sure sign of the rejection of woman to come. Adam could not outright blame God (although it surely sounded like he wanted to), but he could blame Eve. Although God had commanded Adam not to eat from the tree (v. 17), he barely took any responsibility when his disobedience was discovered.

Adam admitted he ate from the tree only to suggest it was Eve's fault that he did. At that moment, man conveniently forgot that God had joined him and woman together as one. Adam saw himself as separate from Eve, whom he had called the bone of his bones and flesh of his flesh (Gen. 2:23). This was the moment Adam decided to look out for number one—himself. He lacked both sympathy and support for Eve, even in the presence of God. This was probably one of the first signs of the true nature of man.

Eve must have felt awful. God was angry with her, and her husband practically disowned her in God's presence. But Eve and Adam had something in common: they both played the blame game. She blamed the serpent, and Adam blamed her and God. Whatever level of responsibility they each had, they blamed their problems on someone or something else. It's no wonder that sinful acts lead mankind to cast blame instead of repent.

As history has so shown, man continues to rule over woman even to this day. Women continue to strive for equality on the job regarding pay, assignments, recognition, equal rights, and fair treatment. Nevertheless, God did not create woman just for man. The Bible says He created woman to be a helper comparable to man (vv 20-24). Being female may suggest to some that women are not as smart relative to men. However, we are just as relevant as men.

Woman was made from the rib of a man. This was personal space—an area not far from Adam's heart. God went within man and took a part out of him to create woman. This demonstrates that man should give of himself first. Woman being created from man's rib automatically made them one. She did not come from the earth as he did; she came directly from his body. They were to be one in covenant as Adam had suggested, bone of his bone (v. 23), but they were also to be one in spirit. What was in Adam was reflected in who Eve was and what she did. Eve did not make Adam eat from the Tree of Knowledge because the desire to do so was already in him, which is why she first ate. She followed what she knew.

God Provided the Man to Provide for the Woman

God provided for the man. God then used the man to provide for the woman. I believe God was trying to teach Adam something, but Adam missed it the first time around. Adam chose to deflect and reject. He missed the fact that he was responsible for himself and Eve. He was to provide, and if he needed or wanted help, his wife would be there at his side waiting, willing, and wanting. Adam did not meet his responsibility.

Eve wandered off by herself, and the serpent was waiting for her. The serpent did not go to Adam, for he was the one God had given the commandment not to eat from the Tree of Knowledge (Gen. 2:17). The serpent went to Eve. This does not mean women are weaker than men, and it certainly does not mean women have no responsibility. It means that when God joins man and woman together, they are to remain as one. Being one takes covenant and communication. Can two people walk together unless they agree (Amos 3:3)? What caused Eve to be away from Adam at such a convenient time for the serpent? As one who is responsible, Adam should have known where the one for whom he was responsible was at all times. That period of separation led to what sometimes appears to be a permanent distance between man and woman.

Order Provides a Level of Control

Men and women are both made in the likeness of God. A man (or woman) who fails because they refuse to accept responsibility is one who does not know who he (or she) is. Neither have been taught the truth regarding the trust and responsibility God placed into their hands through Adam and Eve. God bestowed upon them some of His characteristics. God, as our provider, is one of the many forms of evidence of His love for us. From the beginning, He tried to mold us into His likeness. Because of a spirit of rejection and selfishness, men and women have failed. Even after Adam claimed Eve was bone of his bone and flesh of his flesh, he failed. His declaration sounded good, but somewhere along the way, he betrayed himself and didn't even know it. We cannot love God or others completely when we do not know how to love ourselves.

How is it that Adam had more responsibility when he and Eve were given equal dominion over the earth? It is because of order. Adam was created first, so he was to behave more responsibly. He chose to go along with what Eve said even though he knew what God had commanded. God is the Father, Son, and Holy Spirit all in one, but each Person of the Trinity has responsibilities and assignments. The Son will not go against the Father, and the Holy Spirit will not go against the Father or the Son. How is it that Adam relinquished his responsibility to Eve when it was God who gave it to him first? That's on Adam. We know this because God said to Adam, "Because you have *heeded* the voice of your wife and have eaten from the tree of which I commanded you saying, 'You shall not eat of it'" (Gen. 3:17). This was a subtle reminder of what the order was supposed to be. God, Adam, and Eve. It was not God, Eve, and Adam. Order would have controlled the situation in the garden with the serpent.

Men and women need each other and are equally important to one another. They are so important that the Word of God says, "He *who* finds a wife finds a good thing and obtains favor from the LORD" (Prov. 18:22). This is more than a compliment to women; it is a note to women who become wives. A *wife* brings favor to her husband by way of her relationship with the Lord. The Bible did not mention anything about a girlfriend or a mistress bringing favor. The verse clearly states: "a wife." So, he who finds the woman chosen for him and makes her his wife not just through a piece of paper but also through a covenant relationship is favored by God.

God's favor is greater than a hook-up, putting in a good word, making connections, or receiving favor from our friends. There is nothing that can top God's favor. Eve did not bring favor to her husband; she brought shame and condemnation. Her disobedience brought chastisement from God and resentment from her husband. Eve was out of order, which led to the situation being out of control.

God Made Her in His Image

Perhaps the results of Eve's disobedience were a part of God's plan. Adam and Eve chose each other—their fleshly desires—over God's commandment. They had disobeyed and put their own desires before God. The irony is that their act of sin is also what turned them against one another.

For Eve, the love of her life, Adam, would be the one to bring the most pain into her life. Maybe this situation would point her back to God because there was nowhere else for her to turn. No one could love her the way God would love her. He knew everything about her. Although God took a bone from Adam, God made Eve in His image. He gave her gifts and authority, and He filled her with love. He would not leave or betray her. God's love for her would become known as *agape* love. His love would last forever (Ps. 118:1).

But Eve was guilty of sin. All mankind originated from her, which was most serious because she was one half of the population at that time. Although God did not destroy Eve, she needed to bear the responsibility of the choice she made. She chose to listen to the enemy instead of obeying God. And God, being who He is, keeps His word. He had told Adam that eating from the tree would surely bring death (Gen. 2:17). God, being merciful and kind, did not bring death upon them immediately. If He had sought only to punish them, He would have struck them down at that moment.

God Made a Place Just for Women

Though Adam and Eve had sinned, their price to pay was minor compared to the debt Christ would pay on the cross. He would eventually pay for their sins, as well as yours and mine. It appeared Eve had almost ruined everything for us. However, God did not allow mankind's destruction. The enemy meant to lead them into disobedience for harm, but God used every bit of the situation for good.

I believe Eve's hurt, suffering, and shame positioned women for God's use. Her trials and tribulations have been seen in the lives of women repeatedly throughout generations. Because God is such a loving Father, His heart never left women. Although He saw our weaknesses through Eve, He acknowledged our strengths.

God made a place just for women. After all, what man wants to endure the pain of giving birth to children? Yes, women have gone where no man likely wants to go: the labor and delivery room up in stirrups. Remember, men and women are not to be totally independent of one another. We are to work together for the good of one another, this world, and God's Kingdom.

CHAPTER TWO

RELATABLE AND RELEVANT

There are two main characters in Matthew 26:6-13. The first is Jesus Christ, and the second is the woman in Bethany. During this scene, the woman was not beside a man as she stood before God the Son. However, she would not be rejected.

There have been many other women who have worshipped, honored, and supported Jesus in their own ways. There were the women who had been healed of evil spirits and different diseases. Women like Mary Magdalene, of whom Jesus casted seven demons out, and others provided for Jesus out of their own resources (Luke 8:2-3).

There was something different about the woman in Bethany. She functioned in a much-needed role specifically chosen by God. She functioned as a woman. She did not need to prove anything. She did not need a degree, title, or position in the community. She just needed to be a woman. Isn't God good?!

God made both man and woman equally in His image. He blessed both and gave them the same authority (Gen. 1:27-28). Although we live in a society where men and women go back and forth about equality, God intentionally chose a woman from Bethany to go and anoint His Son, Jesus Christ, in the presence of men. God does nothing by accident; He does not make mistakes. Everything God does is according to His will.

Women Were Made to Fit Right In

In the book of Genesis, God seemingly interacted more with Adam than He did with Eve in the beginning. This is possible potentially because Adam was made before Eve, allowing God to bond with him first. When Eve and Adam ate the fruit and hid themselves in the garden, it was Adam to whom God called out (Gen. 3:8-9). His questions were directed toward Adam, whom He had given the commandment to first. The importance of the situation helped to determine the order in which God operated in the relationship.

Jesus operated in the same manner with His disciples and the woman in Bethany. Although the disciples questioned the purpose of the anointing, Jesus did not feel the need to place their concern above the woman's purpose. Therefore, it appears Jesus related to the woman in Bethany more than He did to the disciples who had spent the past few years with Him. The significance of the woman's assignment in Bethany was most likely at the forefront of Jesus' mind. She was performing a task that could not have happened any other way except through womanhood. Jesus operated in the order of what was most relevant at the time.

As humans, it is important that we at least try to understand the relevance of being made in the image of God. Hopefully this will encourage a person to do his or her best to walk in this privilege. Were we made just to look good? Were we made to have an abundance of things here on earth? If that's so, why were we made as spiritual beings? Spiritual beings do not need things. This is possibly why Adam and Eve, in the beginning, did not own clothing or other material things. Before God breathed into the nostrils of man, he had not come to life yet. Man was nothing more than an empty shell. It is our spirit that gives us life in the image of God and allows us to relate to God, who is Spirit. And it is the Spirit that causes us to remain relevant in God's spiritual Kingdom. God our Father is looking for those who will worship Him in spirit and truth (John 4:23-24). This is about having and understanding the ability to access the Kingdom and relate to God on His terms. Studying your Bible is a way to learn about the Lord, how He relates to us, and how to relate to Him.

One day, a lawyer asked Jesus what the greatest commandment was (Matt. 22:36). This man was of the Pharisees, a religious group who believed more in keeping the law of Moses than submitting to God *because* of the law. They thought by simply keeping the law, they were safe from destruction. The law, which included the commandments, were established to teach mankind how to relate to God and how to treat others. If this was accomplished, it was seen as obedience to God, which led to the true worship of God. This, in turn, becomes evidence of our love for God.

Jesus, however, did not make any reference to any of the commandments that could be made into rituals by mankind. Instead, Jesus answered, "... 'You shall love the Lord your God with all your heart, with all your soul, and with all your mind'" (v. 37). Jesus led with the commandment that keeps God first and requires man to interact with God through obedience. Anyone can be religious, never relating to God personally. But in the interest of being relatable and relevant to the Kingdom of God, one must be willing and able to submit heart, mind, and soul to God.

One of the foundations of God's Kingdom is love. He rules with love. Love is a clear representation of who God is. Love is the bond that keep us under God's grace and mercy. Without love, it is difficult to operate under God's terms, especially if one's flesh is the dominant participant, which leads to the reason why God is looking for those who will worship Him in spirit and truth. Too often, people try to act out or practice their way into relating to God. This is something you might do when meeting another person. God requires that you approach Him—spirit to Spirit—with truthful hearts, minds, and souls. The first step is being yourself. You need not try and relate to God the way someone else does. Set yourself apart and relate on God's terms. You may be criticized for it; nevertheless, it is your relationship with the Lord.

While the disciples criticized the woman in Bethany as she poured the perfumed oil on Jesus, she did not say a word. She did not need to defend herself. Her strength of heart and unwavering mind revealed she believed more about who Jesus was than the men sitting around Him. She was able to engage Him in this activity while she came under verbal assault. Jesus could see the woman in Bethany was serious about what she went there to do. Perhaps the disciples could not see it, but this woman was relevant and so was her work.

The Reason Women Are Relevant Is in the Scriptures

God first must be relevant in our lives. If He's irrelevant to us, how can we understand our own relevance? If we don't see ourselves as people needing to be delivered, saved, and set free from bondage, how can we see God as Lord and Savior? For mankind to see God as relevant, we must come into agreement with what He says about us. We put God first by committing to a covenant relationship with Him. The beauty of this is that we enter a place of blessings as we walk in agreement with Him—with obedience comes blessings (Deut. 28:1-14).

The relevance of women is written in the scriptures. When God made woman, He said it was because man did not have a helper like himself (Gen. 2:18-22). God referred to the woman as a helper. This does not take anything away from who a woman is. God saw it as a compliment then and continues to see it as that today. Without the woman even doing anything, God described her as possessing one of His characteristics. In the book of John, the third Person of the Holy Trinity is called the Helper; His work is seen throughout the Old and New Testaments.

Knowing that the Holy Spirit is the Helper puts us (women) in the best of company. Jesus said to His disciples, "But the Helper, the Holy Spirit, whom the Father will send in My name, He will teach you all things, and bring to your remembrance all things that I said to you" (John 14:26). The Holy Spirit would uphold everything Jesus taught His disciples and would teach them as well. He would remain with those to whom Jesus had chosen to share the gospel and advance the Kingdom of God.

As helpers created by God, we are to continue to advance His love, goodness, and image in all things. Just as Eve was to help Adam do well, we are to do likewise today: "... For everyone to whom much is given, from him much will be required ..." (Luke 12:48).

Being Relevant Is of God

In fulfilling our purposes, we must always be mindful that we are to do everything as to the Lord (Col. 3:23). Whatever task He may assign, we should do it with all our heart, knowing that our work is to help bring that assignment to completion and honor the Lord's name. We shall not take our assignments for granted, neither shall we look down on our position as helpers. It is of God's own character in which we were designed.

Do not focus on your circumstances, where you are from, or your family bloodline. This has nothing to do with you being relevant. Too often, when a child is born, worldly garments are piled on them—from which family member they look like to the finest clothes for them to wear. Very little, if anything, is said about the spirit of the child, who they are, and who they will become. From the time a child is conceived, the mother, father, and other responsible loved ones should say blessings over him or her while the child is in the womb. They can hear you. Say to the child, "You are blessed because you are made in the image of God."

When God decided to make man, He indicated how it was to be done. He said, "... Let Us make man in Our image, according to Our likeness ..." (Gen. 1:26). God intentionally made us just like Himself—all three Persons. Jesus coming down from heaven covered in flesh demonstrated the God-given potential of man.

When God made Adam and Eve, He showed them and told them of the blessings around them. Then He spoke blessings over them and encouraged them to walk in the authority He had given to them (Gen. 1-2).

As God led Moses to bring the children of Israel out of Egypt, they were transitioning from bondage to freedom, and their lives would be totally different from what they had known before. Through Moses, God informed them of the results of obedience and disobedience. This transition was more than a lateral move; there was a covenant and some blessings attached.

God said to Jeremiah, "'Before I formed you in the womb, I knew you; Before you were born I sanctified you; I ordained you a prophet to the nations'" (Jer. 1:5). This should leave all of us without complaints about our parents, the stock we come from, or our past.

In every situation, God provided what man needed even before man needed it. This is how meaningful life is to God. Your success is important to Him—so important that He has already set things in place for it to happen. It is a matter of your perception and which way you choose to go. Choose that which is relevant and not that which only looks good.

You Are Greater than What You See and Capable of Much More than What You Know

Focus on the image of whom you were created. Learn to be intentionally mindful about it. It does not matter that you look just like your Daddy or that you are the spitting image of your Mama. We are all made in the image of God, so who we are goes beyond DNA. It is a spiritual matter. You are greater than what you see and capable of doing much more than what you know. Your Father in heaven is not limited. However, we have been trained by mankind that we are limited. A man trains himself not to go beyond a certain point, then he trains others to not think beyond that point either. While we have God's spiritual DNA, we are not all the same.

If a puppy is raised by a couple of cats, that does not make him a cat. He must take notice that there is something different about him and his "parents." When he takes note of this and begins to explore the difference, he will then look for others like him.

When systems are set in place to capture a particular group and their performance is used only to point out their failures, those systems will only keep that group in bondage. They will think they must somehow measure up to other groups to become successful in life. This is not true. If God created everyone to be doctors, most of the world would fail. And if the puppy grows up thinking he is a cat, the first time he jumps off a roof will probably be his last.

You are relevant as you are because you are made in the image of God. Mankind may judge, ridicule, and demean you, but you were not made by man. If you should lose focus of this, remember God's love for you is unconditional. His love never changes. Man changes, but God never will.

We Must Agree with God About Everything

The woman in Bethany was a helper to Jesus. She was mindful of one thing: the work to be done. She did not have any companions along to help her, yet she was determined. She approached this task as an honor, for it was her desire to worship the Son of God. To God the Father, she was on an assignment. To Jesus, her act was seen as a good work. In all aspects, she associated her work with who Jesus was to her.

Agree with God. Accept and responsibly use everything He has given to you. All is useful for His Kingdom and His glory. We are to bring glory to His name.

CHAPTER THREE

BE MINDFUL

The woman in Bethany went and anointed Jesus, although it seemed she had little knowledge about why she had to do it. Eve, however, received the commandment from God not to eat off the tree, yet she failed to follow what God said. How is it that those who walked and talked with God were not mindful enough to follow His commands, but the woman in Bethany who had never seen Him completed her assignment without fail?

Both women faced challenges; Eve faced the serpent, and the woman in Bethany ultimately faced some unsuspecting foes. Both were given a challenge by the enemy, not God. The challenge to Eve was tempting because it offered personal gain. How could she pass up eating the fruit that looked so delicious or pass up becoming like God? She could have had both just by eating the snack from the tree. Sound familiar? The woman in Bethany saw nothing to gain other than to anoint Jesus. Perhaps once Eve conceived the idea of being like God, the potential of what she could become became more important than what God had commanded her. When one's focus is on oneself, he or she appears to be more vulnerable to distractions and harm.

A Mind Able to Discern in the Spirit Is a Mind Not Controlled by Distractions

Being able to focus is good. Being able to control what we focus on is better. The moment the enemy spoke to Eve, he had her attention and her mind. He did this by calling her attention to something familiar to her. The serpent said to Eve, "Has God indeed said, 'You shall not eat of every tree of the garden?'" (Gen. 3:1) Well, this sounded *close* to what God had said. Eve repeated what God said regarding the trees of the garden, so the problem wasn't that she did not know. The problem was she felt compelled to answer the enemy. Before this scene, Eve only answered to Adam and to God. Eve did not allow herself time to think about who she was speaking with. She was distracted, and the enemy knew this. He caught her attention by appearing to help her understand what God really said, which would aid him in reaching his goal of sowing disobedience into mankind.

It is easy to be in a relationship with God but go off the rails when one is seemingly under pressure. The woman in Bethany withstood the pressure applied when she went to anoint Jesus. Regardless of what the enemy says or what our own minds try to tell us, we must follow God. Being focused allows us to hear, see, and discern what is true. A mind that can discern in the spirit is a mind not controlled by distractions. A sound mind has the ability to rise above the noise, doubts, questions, and fears.

This was unlike Jesus' disciples. When Jesus had spoken to them regarding His pending crucifixion, they seemed distracted. Peter, who often had some sort of response to Jesus, said nothing. Were they not prepared for what was to come? Did they not understand? Jesus had told them about His impending crucifixion before. He said the words "you know," which suggests that this was not their first time hearing this information. It could also mean He was reminding them so they would be aware of their surroundings. After all, this was a busy time because the people were preparing to observe the feast of Passover. His disciples could have easily become distracted by everything else going on. And it appears they were distracted.

Set Your Mind on What Is Sustainable

There are so many things that could have been going through their minds. Yet, Jesus wanted them to focus. He needed them to be alert. He wanted them to be mindful. Jesus was and remains the perfect example for teaching us how to stay focused and fight distraction. One day, the Holy Spirit led Jesus up into the wilderness to be tested by the devil. Jesus fasted for forty days and forty nights. The Bible says that after Jesus had fasted, He was hungry. Then, Satan appeared to test Jesus. The first thing the devil brought up was the very thing *he thought* would be on Jesus' mind: food (Matt. 4).

The enemy tried to do to Jesus what he did to Adam and Eve. He attempted to play a mind game. The enemy's first attack is on the mind. If he can instill doubt, fear, paranoia, or other uncertainties in one's mind, he will gain room to roam. The enemy wants us to overthink. When we start overthinking, we start overanalyzing, which leads to questioning, doubt, and fear.

Knowing that Jesus was hungry, the enemy attempted to make hunger the focus of Jesus' attention. He used food—which he perceived Jesus wanted—to distract and tempt Him away from His Father. Satan's desire was to determine what Jesus would think about and eventually do. The enemy wants to control your mind so that he can control you.

Satan did not know that Jesus had chosen to set His mind on sustainable things. Because of this, Satan had no real power over Jesus. But Jesus the Son of God could not allow flesh to enter the equation because it would become a distraction that could lead to bondage. Every time the enemy tried to persuade Jesus to think on a tempting offer, Jesus turned to the one source that was more reliable than thoughts and opinions: the Word of God. He drew His strength from the Word of God—His foundation. Jesus said, "Heaven and earth will pass away, but My words will by no means pass away" (Matt. 24:35). His words will never fail, and Jesus is the Word.

Be Present

Just like Jesus was led into the wilderness, the woman in Bethany was led to an unsuspecting area. By her actions, she had one goal in mind: go and anoint Jesus. She had to perform a task that was not only going to take courage but would need a set, strengthened mind. She would have to remain cool under the circumstances because the place God was sending her to get to Jesus would become a battlefield. It would not be a physical fight, but it would be one for control of her mind. Her thinking process and decision-making would be questioned. She would be viewed as having a hidden agenda instead of a Spirit-led purpose.

The woman in Bethany, like Jesus, would have to fight mentally to stay above the comments, questions, and insults hurled at her. Ordinary men weren't going after her. No, the men pursuing her had been following Jesus; they were His disciples.

Their sharp insults were not only hurled at the woman in Bethany, but they propelled Jesus to enter in the battle to fight for her. Even as Jesus entered in, she remained present remembering why she was there and what she was doing. She did not let up because she was focused on her purpose. She wasn't there for personal gain; she was there for Jesus.

Our minds significantly impact how we perform in life. If we allow distractions to derail us, our accomplishments might be few, if any. But if we push forward, we can realize some of our biggest dreams. Sometimes we don't see the traps the enemy sets before us and walk right into them. If you see them, why walk into them? Focus and be clear about what you want to do. Be mindful.

Stay Prayed-Up

While we do not have any definitive statement that the woman in Bethany had prayed before entering Simon the Leper's place, we can use deductive reasoning to infer that at some point, she believed anointing Jesus was the right thing to do, and therefore she did it. She also needed to tell someone in some way what she was about to do.

Her thoughts were not conveyed to man. The woman in Bethany had been talking with the Lord. This is believed because Jesus was not at all caught off-guard. His disciples were, but Jesus was expecting her to come to that home. There are times when we must have more than a good idea. We need the Lord to support what He has placed within us. This comes through prayer.

Prayer can take on different forms. Some people believe in praying audibly to God. Others believe in simply mouthing the words without sound. Then there are others who pray spirit to Spirit. Their hearts are conveyed to God without ever opening their mouths. Any form of prayer is fine. The key is to communicate with the Lord.

Jesus did this often. He stayed in touch with God the Father. Jesus received guidance, direction, love, and support, as well as strength from the Father. We can have great ideas, but we must stay prayed up, placing our entire being and all that we have in the Lords' hands.

It would have been foolish for the woman in Bethany to have gone into a place such as Simon the Leper's house without prayer. We cannot win against the enemy using our natural minds. The enemy is not flesh; he is a spirit. Fighting against powers of darkness requires the will and ways of God (Eph. 6:12). We need the Word of God. His Word is power.

Jesus was given all power in heaven and on earth (Matt. 28:18). As we trust and follow Him, we too can walk in power. This is true. The more one walks by faith, the more powerful she or he becomes. This kind of faith is rarely seen these days, but Moses, Noah, Elijah, the woman in Bethany, Mary Magdalene, and others walked this way. Through faith, they did things that other people would not have even imagined. They kept their eyes on the Lord, and we are to do the same.

Tests and trials will come for us just like they did for Jesus. We are responsible for awareness wherever we go, what we say, and what we do. We must choose to use this power to make good decisions: "Let this mind be in you which was also in Christ Jesus," (Phil. 2:5).

Love Can Change Things

God has given us power through His Word, which will never fail. He has also given us love. It is because of His love that Jesus bore all things on the cross. John 3:16 says, "For God so loved the world that He gave His only begotten Son, that whoever believes in Him should not perish but have eternal life."

I am a firm believer that God loves me. Despite myself, I know God loves me. The Bible clearly states it was because of God's love for us that He sent Jesus, His Son, to die for us. Once I came to this conclusion, my mind and life began to be transformed. Fear went away. I have no doubt that accepting God's love set my mind free from bondage: "There is no fear in love; but perfect love casts out fear ..." (1 John. 4:18).

God's love is unconditional, and once you accept the fact that God loves you regardless of any wrong you may have done, you too will experience freedom from guilt, shame, and blame. Your mind will become clearer, and your life will be transformed. This is because God's love transcends all barriers, traumas, and sin. There is nothing that can keep Him from loving you. There is no end to God's love.

The day Jesus died on the cross, love changed the atmosphere. The earth quaked, the dead got up, and the curtain in the temple was torn from top to bottom (Matt. 27:50-53). Love has the ability to change things and people—dead or alive—over time. Because of this love, we will one day see the face of Jesus Christ.

People sometimes believe love must be felt because that is what most are familiar with. We have been led to believe love is about a feeling. However, the results of love can be seen in individual lives, neighborhoods, and communities. God's love must first be received by faith. You may not necessarily feel His presence like that of your parent or children. Because you can see them and touch them, the experience is different. Therefore, you must believe by faith that His love for you is real. God is Spirit, and you are spirit. Commune with Him spirit to Spirit. He has given you a spirit of love.

One might ask, how can God love us? By being Himself. God is love (1 John. 4:7-8); therefore, when you were made in His image, you were filled with His love. This enables you to love God, yourself, and others.

I can only imagine the woman in Bethany when she saw the face of Jesus. She saw the essence of love. Jesus represented the Kingdom of God, and He was the representation of love. It was the love of Jesus that drew the woman in Bethany, as well as many others. His love caused her to act upon what she knew was right to do. The commandment to love God with all our heart, mind, soul, and strength isn't just for the Lord. It is so we can have the purest relationship possible with our Father in heaven. God does not want part of us. He wants all of us. This love changes one from the inside out. Settle this in your mind. You are loved.

The Things of God Are Spiritually Discerned

The things of God are spiritually discerned. There were times when God spoke directly to His prophets, telling them what to say and do. Sometimes, they were led by the Holy Spirit. Today, some of us are led by the Holy Spirit because we do not hear God speak to us directly as He did to others in the Bible. So, we tune in mindfully to our inner spirits to hear from His Spirit.

It was likely the Holy Spirit who prompted the woman in Bethany to go to Jesus, and it is amazing that she had the mind to go. It was not of her own doing because the Bible mentions nothing of her having a conversation with Jesus. However, it appeared as if He may have been expecting her. The Bible also mentions nothing of her explaining what she was doing, which indicates she did not go in with her own agenda. It appears she just went in and did what she knew she had to do. In her mind, her intentions were not about her. It was about Jesus Christ. Despite insults and questions swirling around her, she operated with a discerning spirit, believing it was necessary to complete the task.

When it comes to the Kingdom of God, assignments and lessons are not always obvious. Because the Kingdom is spiritual, we cannot always expect to see it with the natural eye or hear it with the natural ear, neither will we always understand it with a natural mind. We must be open to the Spirit of God to receive the things of God: "But the natural man does not receive the things of the Spirit of God, for they are foolishness to him; nor can he know them, because they are spiritually discerned" (1 Cor. 2:14).

The woman in Bethany was focused on a mission, yet she had no control or say about whether Jesus would see her. She went into the house because she had the mind to, possessed the power to, and operated with the love of God. She followed His Spirit.

Knowing that we have been given a sound mind with the power and love of God should encourage all of us. We should be empowered to do great things just as the Apostle Paul wrote: "I can do all things through Christ who strengthens me" (Phil. 4:13). The key is remembering who strengthens us. For God has not given us a spirit of fear, but of power, and of love, and of a sound mind (2 Tim. 1:7). Be mindful and be present. Be of a sound mind.

CHAPTER FOUR

RELIGION BUT NO RELATIONSHIP

I remember as a child when a stranger walked up to a relative of mine and stated they were a distant cousin of our family. And as soon as we were far enough away from the person, my relative said, "We're no relation to them." She did not hesitate to make sure that I did not accept what the person had said.

While teaching His disciples, Jesus explained to them that not everyone who calls on His name has a relationship with Him. Even if they say things to sound like they belong to Him or perform acts to look like they belong to Him, Jesus said He will say to them, "... 'I never knew you ...'" (Matt. 7:23).

Jesus was direct and straight to the point with His disciples. He wanted them to know it was not so much what they said or did, but what truly mattered was what was in their hearts. Religion comes from practice. Relationships come from the heart. Jesus is looking for righteous living. While most people know how to live right, some choose to do wrong.

During the time that Jesus came onto the earth, many people practiced religion. Maybe it was something like what people do today. Some practice for when they get to heaven, but this is not a rehearsal. This is the time to have a real relationship with the Lord.

To have a real relationship with the Lord, one must be involved with Him. There must be a connection between the two—a common ground. This common ground is Jesus Christ. Part of His coming was to reestablish a loving relationship between God and man. That is why John 3:16 clearly states, "For God so loved the world, that He gave His only begotten Son." This is Jesus. Jesus is the gift of love. His love for the Father led Him to give His life for those who would believe He is the Son of God. This is a powerful love. So powerful, the Bible says, "Above all things have fervent love for one another, for 'love will cover a multitude of sins'" (1 Peter 4:8).

Because of the sinful nature of mankind, some people behave as if they are afraid of God. God is to be feared through reverence because He is worthy, not scary. His love for us is not to control us but to be in a relationship with us and share with us all the blessings He created for us. He tried to do this for Adam and Eve through relationship, but Adam and Eve failed. And man keeps on failing, even today. Many fails at relationship.

It appears that religion has taken hold of some people. Just because the efforts or experiences feel good, that doesn't mean they are pleasing to God. You can have a preaching, singing, and shouting good time in the building and leave with the same empty heart. And midweek, you may find yourself desiring something more because the good feelings wear off. The presence of God in our lives never wears off. That is religion, and the cycle repeats itself. Like getting high on a drug (so I have been told), religion is a feeling, not a way of life. God is not about just feelings. He is about sustainable results. He cares about you and what you go through. However, you must be all-in, all day and every day, regardless of what you're feeling.

Think about your relationship with your spouse or other family members and friends. You do not have the same conversation with them every time you talk with them. You most likely share the latest updates with them each time you speak. God wants you to share these things with Him as well. He wants to be included in your life. God loves you and wants a real relationship with you.

I am not sure if the woman in Bethany was religious, but I would say she probably was not. I say this because she went to the person of Jesus. It was the person she was interested in. This was not so much what her daily rituals were or might have been. She made a successful attempt to see Him face to face. This is the relationship we should be after. We should not stop until we have that spirit-to-Spirit relationship with God—nothing or no one between us and Him.

This is important because religion can be used to control individuals, depending on their perception of it. Women were sometimes viewed as being "lesser" than men at this time. The woman in Bethany associated with Jesus Christ, not with what others thought or believed. While women were considered weaker than men, her action showed her strength. She engaged Jesus because of her belief in Him.

Too often, tradition takes precedence in who the Lord is and how we interact with Him. One of the wonderful things about being in a relationship with the true and living God is that He is so awesome, and He will occasionally show you who He is. In those rare moments, I feel like a little kid being shown something spectacular for the first time. His ways literally blow me away. It takes a moment to get myself back together. He wants to show us His ways, and He wants a personal relationship with each of us.

To develop this relationship, some may ask where God is. How do we get to Him? You do not have to go looking for God; He will come to you. One day while in the desert, Moses saw a bush burning, but it was not being consumed by the fire. Well, this got Moses' attention. So, God spoke from the bush to Moses. God met Moses right where Moses was physically and spiritually.

Moses got to see a small portion of God's power. God speaking to Moses from the burning bush foreshadowed the kind of relationship He and Moses would have. He used His power a great deal in Moses' life because of what He had called Moses to do. Because of Moses' self-doubt, he needed encouragement and constant reassurance as his relationship with the Lord grew. By engaging Moses in such ways, God left little room for doubt in Moses' mind about who He was and is, the God of Abraham, Isaac, and Jacob (Exod. 3:1-8).

God knows exactly what you need. It's not about your education, where you grew up, or your family background. He knows your skills, strengths, and weaknesses. God is interested in having a fruitful, loving, and thriving relationship with *you*.

Religion Rejects; Christ Embraces

One of the wonderful things about being in relationship with the true and living God is that He is not an object hanging on a chain. He is not a stone or piece of wood. He is not a figurine sitting on a shelf that we must dust off. God is the only true, living, Supreme Spiritual being. He is the Creator of heaven, the earth, and all that is within them. Also, He can be at any place in any span of time. Yes, He can be with you and all His other children at the same time. You do not have to schedule an appointment or wait in line. He is always available and closer than you think.

The Lord can communicate with anyone. However, there is a huge difference between religion and relationships. What took place with Abraham, Isaac, Jacob, and Moses was all about relationships. However, things were different with the patriarch of the family. Terah, the father of Abraham, worshipped idols. This was Terah's religion, which would explain why God told Abraham to leave his father's house. Traditional religion tends to be limiting. It can be about one—one kind or oneself. A relationship is about everyone involved. Traditional religion has the tendency to reject, but Christ embraces us when we have a relationship with Him. Abraham had to reject his father's religion to become the patriarch of many people.

Embracing others does not mean you have to like their ways or vice versa. Jesus' disciples did not have to like the fact that the woman in Bethany came in to anoint Jesus, but they had to live with it. What she did was not their way, but that did not matter. It was God's way of doing things that mattered.

God states that our ways are not His ways (Isa. 55:8). None of us are exactly the people He desires us to be. All of us fall short of walking in the ways of God. Therefore, no one can claim that their way is the best. As we walk in relationship with Jesus Christ, we learn to embrace others through the love of Christ. I believe this is what Christ wants His disciples to understand. Being made in the image of God should enable us to relate to Him and to one another, whether we agree or disagree. While the woman in Bethany did not fit the description of what Jesus' disciples thought a wise person should behave like, she carried on with her assignment.

Women are often overlooked when it comes to assignments. Some might think the assignments are only fitting for men. However, Jesus chose to meet some women right where they were. On the day that Mary Magdalene and the other Mary went to the tomb hoping to care for Jesus body, an angel appeared and told them Jesus had risen. The women were instructed to go and tell Jesus' disciples and to meet Him in Galilee (Matt. 28:5-7). As they went on their way to tell the disciples, they ran into Jesus, and He told them the same thing (vv 8-10). Jesus knew where His disciples were; therefore, He could have gone to them Himself. But He intentionally gave these women the right to deliver the good news of His resurrection first, and He made sure that the first to hear the good news from these women were His disciples.

Jesus chose to embrace these women, and He gave them the assignment to carry the gospel. If Jesus only wanted to use men, He had eleven He could have gone to and given the authority to first. But He chose to work with those who had not only walked into a relationship with Him but who demonstrated that the relationship had not ended just because He had been crucified. Their faith in Him led their hearts to believe they could do more for Him, even if it was only to care for His body.

Sometimes those right in front of us may look different when compared to ourselves and, therefore, seem like anything other than an obvious choice or solution. For this reason, people reject others over misconceptions. This is not of God. This is a defect of human nature, and it is usually based on some sort of fear. In other words, there is no real reason, but people will make one up.

Jesus does not judge us based on the way we look. He does not judge us based on the color of our skin. And He did not judge the women when they met Him in the garden near His tomb. Jesus looks at the heart of the person. His desire to have a relationship with us benefits *us*. To be embraced by God is almost incomprehensible. We are not worthy, yet He deemed us worthy when Jesus died on the cross for us. He took our place on the cross. Christ embraces.

Jesus knew and understood what women experienced by just being women. Just like some of these women, Jesus was rejected, betrayed, deserted, judged, and mistreated, among other things. He knew what it felt like to have the world against Him. What's even more traumatizing was that this treatment did not come from everyday people; Jesus was rejected by religious leaders.

Religion Can Lead to Blindness

Jesus' life was not threatened by thieves and murderers. Matthew 26:3-4 reads, "Then the chief priests, the scribes, and the elders of the people assembled at the palace of the high priest, who was called Caiaphas, and plotted to take Jesus by trickery and kill *Him*." They were religious folks—spiritual leaders of the people. That's right. They were leading the people astray. They so willingly rejected the Son of God who came representing the Kingdom of God, yet they claimed to have a relationship with God.

The council was made up of Pharisees and Sadducees, and they were not buying Jesus' profession that He was the Son of God. The Pharisees practically worshipped the law by holding traditions in high regard. They sought praise and respect as they zealously kept the law, but they were hypocrites. They looked down on those who, in their eyes, sinned and fell short. So, they kept themselves separate from others who were not like them, failing to realize they, too, fell short of God's standards (Matt. 23:23).

The Sadducees did not believe in the resurrection (Acts 23:8). To them, there was no afterlife. They even went as far as to question Jesus about one woman and the seven brothers she married after each one's death (Mark 12:18-27). But Jesus' response, as always, was direct and to the question at hand. Jesus said to them,

> "'Are you not therefore mistaken, because you do not know the scriptures nor the power of God? For when they rise from the dead, they neither marry nor are given in marriage, but are like angels in heaven. But concerning the dead, that they rise, have you not read in the book of Moses, in the *burning* bush *passage*, how God spoke to him, saying, "I am the God of Abraham, the God or Isaac, and the God of Jacob"? He is not the God of the dead, but the God of the living. You are therefore greatly mistaken.'"

> – Mark 12:24-27

Jesus warned His disciples about the ways of the Pharisees and Sadducees (Matt. 16:1-6). Their teachings and beliefs were far off from what Jesus' teaching seemed to interfere with what they believed and their way of living. Caiaphas, who was the high priest in the temple during the time Jesus was ministering, also opposed Jesus and His teachings. The religious leaders were supposed to be some of the most educated and spiritual people. Yet they carelessly led the common people astray. However, Jesus did not follow their lead; He followed God.

There is no law that proves that any religion makes one closer to God than another. But there is only one God, regardless of your religion, denomination, knowledge, or lack of knowledge about Him. There is only one way to get to God the Father, and that is through Jesus Christ, His Son (John 14:6). Your relationship with Him is personal. God has set the standard for all who wish to commune with Him. Jesus said to the woman at the well, "'God *is* Spirit, and those who worship Him must worship in spirit and truth'" (John 4:24). Jesus did not say she had to worship where the Jews worshipped, but only that it be in spirit and truth.

Jesus shared something with the woman at the well that He had not shared with the spiritual leaders. To worship God in spirit and truth is the purest form of worship. The Father is looking for those who willingly acknowledge His divine nature as the Supreme Spiritual Being, by interacting with Him in their true nature as a spiritual being. We were created to commune with God, spirit to Spirit. Our spirit person is supposed to be our dominant nature because we were made in the image of God.

One day when Jesus' disciples questioned Him about the Father and where He was going, Jesus said it this way. "'I am the way, the truth, and the life. No one comes to the Father except through Me. If you had known Me, you would have known My Father also; and from now on you know Him and have seen Him'" (John 14:6-7). Jesus was in the flesh as man when He spoke with His disciples, yet He understood that His true likeness was closer to God, than it was man. Jesus was in the flesh, but He operated in the Spirit. He walked in Spirit and truth. When we worship in spirit and truth, we are communing with God the Father, Son (Truth), and spirit to Holy Spirit. This is of the most intimate relationship we can have with God. It is the purest form of worship we can have here on earth.

While the Pharisees and Sadducees were religious leaders, they lacked spirituality. They had influence in the temple and in their community, yet they could not see their own individual needs. Jesus once said to His disciples, "'For what profit is it to a man if he gains the whole world, and loses his own soul? Or what will a man give in exchange for his soul?'" (Matt. 16:24) Religion can cause spiritual blindness.

Some of the Pharisees and Sadducees were religious leaders with criminal minds. No, they did not meet in a back room in an alley or empty warehouse. They met at the palace of the chief priest. They were supposed to be men of God, but they were nothing more than a group of men who had an allegiance to a group of religious people (Matt. 26:3). Their duties, loyalties, and commitments were to themselves and their followers, not God. The chief priest held a position of authority, yet he submitted that authority to the will of the people. These religious leaders who rejected Jesus abandoned their spiritual callings—their purposes. They were religious with no relationship with Jesus Christ, and they certainly did not have one with God the Father.

The Bible says that we are liars if we say we love God but hate one another (1 John 4:20). The Pharisees and Sadducees were religious folks who pretended to have a relationship with God the Father even though they hated Jesus, God the Son. Jesus once said to His disciple Phillip, "... 'He who has seen Me has seen the Father ...'" (John 14:9). With that being said, we cannot get to God the Father unless we go through God the Son. Because the two are one, you can't have a relationship with one and not the other.

Everything the religious leaders were supposed to represent had been cast off. However, this was all according to God's plan. Their traditions and their lack of knowledge were the catalysts to bring about God's perfect plan to save mankind. He knew the hatred these men had toward Jesus would be used according to His purpose.

Another lesson to learn from the Pharisees and Sadducees is that people look for leaders. People looked for leaders they could follow and learn from back then, and they look for them today. But it's confusing when you hear a leader say one thing but behave in a completely different way. As a result, people no longer only look for leaders in the Church. Today, some look to various media platforms for influencers they can follow. And some of these influencers have hundreds, thousands, and even millions of followers.

While we may not intentionally lead anyone astray, people are listening and watching. God expects us to share the truth of the gospel of Jesus Christ. And believe it or not, there are people who do not want anything other than the truth. Even if there are some who do not know what they are looking for, they can recognize the truth when they hear it. Jesus said, "'I am the good shepherd; and I know My *sheep* and am known by My own'" (John 10:14). God will draw people if we share the truth of the gospel of Jesus Christ.

The religious leaders feared people would choose Jesus over them. Although the religious leaders had specific training (mostly due to traditions and perhaps some education behind them), Jesus had power and authority. He had nothing to prove because He was and is the Son of God. People not only followed Him but trusted Him.

The religious leaders were too rooted in their traditions. It was easier for them to hold on to what they knew and understood than to trust Jesus and what He said. Jesus offered something new to them, which made them uncomfortable. Mostly, the religious leaders lacked faith. Habitual routines do not require faith. However, living requires having faith every day because we do not know what each day will bring.

Being in a relationship with the Lord requires faith. It takes effort to pray new prayers to God each day; it takes effort not to pray the same prayer every day. But if you do, make sure it is from the heart and not a place of habit. Ask the Lord to teach you what to pray for. In the Kingdom, these are not necessarily material things. But it can be prayer for more of Jesus, Himself. It can be a prayer for more wisdom, knowledge, and understanding about the Kingdom of God. These prayers help to build the relationship between you and the Lord. He wants you to seek after Him. Then everything else will come.

Another religious leader, a Pharisee by the name of Nicodemus, went to Jesus at night, possibly hoping to avoid being seen by others. It was clear Nicodemus had a hunger for something more. Religion was not enough. I like the fact that he knew there had to be more, therefore he went to the source, Jesus Christ. Sometimes we stay in situations that we know aren't good for us. We want more, and we know that we deserve more. Yet, we're afraid to make a change. Nicodemus could not go to his family, neighbors, or friends. So, he went to Jesus at night. You can do the same. Go to Jesus in prayer. He will hear you, and He will answer you. The answer may not come when you want it, but it will come.

Jesus said to Nicodemus that for man to see the Kingdom of God, he must be born again (John 3:3). Nicodemus lacked the faith needed to be born again, so he began to question Jesus. Nicodemus was in a bad place. He had religion, but he needed salvation to enter the kind of relationship Jesus talked about.

The woman in Bethany was not a religious leader. She was not known for being influential in her community. But she had faith in Jesus, and it gave her access to the Lord, which Nicodemus and so many others wanted and needed.

Religion Is Not a Relationship

Religion is not a relationship. The body of Christ is Spirit filled, living, and thriving. And Jesus is the head (Col. 2:9). Believers operate on behalf of the Kingdom of God all over the world. They are not just Baptist, Presbyterian, or Lutheran. They are people of one denomination called faith. They are from all walks of life who hope in Jesus Christ.

Jesus shared a parable with His disciples about a man who gave his servants resources to use while he was out of the country. The man had instructions to go along with the resources. He said to his servants, "... 'Do business till I come'" (Luke 19:13). In other versions, the word "occupy" replaces "do business." This assignment was based on the relationship the man had with his servants. Jesus wants those of us who are in relationship with Him to continue serving until He returns. This way the relationship extends beyond self and continuously flows to others.

Our relationship with the Lord helps to determine whether we will be loyal to Him and His commandments. In any sustaining relationship, there is growth. As we continue to grow, we will engage others and inhabit more of the earth. This is what Jesus wants from His followers. Works, gifts, and talents alone cannot get us into the Kingdom. In this love relationship, we must be obedient, and walk by faith.

A relationship with the Lord can change a person from the inside out. Having access to our Creator gives new meaning to life as we know it. But the relationship must meet certain criteria. Becoming proficient in certain behaviors and routines has nothing to do with being in a relationship with the Lord. Jesus reminds of us of a parable where a Pharisee prayed, "... 'God, I thank You that I am not like other men—extortioners, unjust, adulterers, or even as this tax collector. I fast twice a week; I give tithes of all that I possess'" (Luke 18:11-12). This man had become so proficient in his rituals that he mistook them for a relationship. His sin was pride, one of the seven abominations (Prov. 6:16-19), and he didn't even know it. At least the tax collector admitted his faults. The self-righteous Pharisee did not have a relationship with the Lord, nor did he have any humility.

Transforming Through This Relationship

We must be careful that we do not look upon others in judgment because all our sins are before God. The Bible says, "That if you confess with your mouth the Lord Jesus and believe in your heart that God has raised Him from the dead, you will be saved. For with the heart, one believes unto righteousness, and with the mouth confession is made unto salvation" (Rom. 10:9-10). Proverbs 18:21 further supports this by stating that death and life are in the power of the tongue. So, the tongue speaks life, and the heart reveals a person's true nature. Others will know you by the way you live and the words you speak. Jesus said, "Not everyone who says to Me, 'Lord, Lord,' shall enter the kingdom of heaven, but he who does the will of My Father in heaven" (Matt. 7:21). Since we are made in the image of God, our lives should reflect it.

God teaches us through His Word how to relate to Him, as well as how to live on this earth along with others. Jesus taught His disciples how to approach God through prayer (Matt. 6). The Spirit of God will guide, teach, and help you, so you should be careful not to ignore or suppress Him. God does not communicate the same way all the time. Seek His face, not just His blessings. Be intentional about getting to know Him and form a loving relationship with Him. Talk with, worship, praise, love, trust, and obey Him. He can be and will be everything you will ever need in life.

God Is Omnipotent

Our relationships with the Lord are based on our faith and confession of belief in Him. This relationship can take us to the mountaintop just like Moses. It can reveal things only God knows and sees, but that depends on our faith and active participation. Jesus said, "... 'If anyone loves Me, he will keep My word; and My Father will love him, and We will come to him and make Our home with him'" (John 14:23). The Lord seeks a relationship with us, but remember, He is the Lord God Almighty. Enter His presence with reverence, for He is holy and righteous. He's not "your boy." He is God.

There is no one like the Lord. Time, units of measurements, degrees, value, computations, or assessments—none of these or anything else can apply to God. He is not limited in any way. He is omnipotent. His power and authority never run out. There is no beginning nor end to who He is. Nothing can stop Him or get in the way of His ruling, yet He is not boastful or arrogant. He does not display His power for show, or to control us.

God gives each of us power and control over our lives. We have the right to choose to live for Him or not. If we do not choose Him, the path leads to death. However, God does not use His power to instill fear or intimidate us. His power sustains, protects, and provides for us.

God's power can change the course of our lives at any moment if we begin to speak and believe it by faith. Being in a relationship with the Lord enables us to do good works. It will make us wonder, *How did I get here?* We can have a loving relationship with this God—the omnipotent God.

God Is Omniscient

God is also omniscient, so we cannot hide anything from Him because He knows everything. Whatever you do or speak in the dark, He knows it. He saw it before you did it. He knew it before you thought it. Jesus knew how His disciples would react to the woman in Bethany. He knew every thought that entered their minds.

As you grow in relationship with the Lord, His Spirit leads and guides you away from thoughts not pleasing to Him. Because He is all-knowing, you need not worry about your future. He knows why each of us was created, and His Spirit attempts to lead us in the direction we should go and therefore allowing us to fulfill our purposes. God gives us dreams to show us who we can become, and He gives us gifts and talents to help us reach those goals. At times when we get off course, it is not surprising to God. He understands we are human, and He does not condemn us. When we repent and ask forgiveness, He puts us right back on track to keep moving toward our destinies.

It is good to have someone in your life that knows everything about you—someone who is willing to help you get to the best place in life. Our Father, the omniscient God, is that someone. The Lord loves you and wants the best for you, so He guides you in the areas you know nothing about. God spoke to His servant Jeremiah saying, "'Call to Me, and I will answer you, and show you great and mighty things, which you do not know'" (Jer. 33:3). In this relationship, put your trust in God because He knows what you need and when you need it.

God Is Omnipresent

You cannot go anywhere that God isn't present. The woman in Bethany might have felt alone, but God was with her. He is everywhere. David said, "'Where can I go from Your Spirit? Or where can I flee from Your presence? If I ascend into heaven, You *are* there; if I make my bed in hell, behold You *are there*'" (Ps. 139:7-8). David was saying that God was wherever he went. This is because God is omnipresent. Because God created everything, He is everywhere and in everything.

One day while working in a hospital, I met a patient who was about to be discharged. I have met thousands of patients in my career as a nurse, but occasionally, I would meet one who somehow lingered in my spirit. With this particular man, it seemed like our paths were supposed to cross. I remember his face vividly because half of it was gone. He had been involved in a drug deal gone wrong. This patient referred to himself as a "mule" during the transaction. He explained how the other guy put a shotgun to his head and pulled the trigger. The patient stated he lay on the ground; aware he had just been shot. The person who shot him, realizing he was not dead, put the shotgun to his head again and attempted to fire. The gun jammed, and the shooter took off.

I don't remember how this man got to the hospital, but I remember him confessing that God was with him that day without even a hint of doubt in his voice. Even in the midst of his criminal activities, he knew God was with him. It is amazing what God can do when you know that He can be anywhere at any time, even if you're somewhere you should not be or doing something you should not do. God is there. The patient left his life as a mule behind to start sharing what the Lord had done for him with others. Praise God!

This world is a big place, and it is easy for us to get lost along the way. Even those who have navigated their way in this world for eighty, ninety, or one hundred years will tell you the Lord has been with them. In your relationship with Him, you can be sure that He will be with you all the way if you abide in Him and allow Him to abide in you: "'And the Lord, He is the One who goes before you. He will be with you, He will not leave you nor forsake you; do not fear nor be dismayed'" (Deut. 31:8). God is omnipresent. He will be with you wherever you go if you let Him.

God being omnipotent, omniscient, and omnipresent reminds me of the words He uses to describe Himself. When God was sending Moses to deliver the children of Israel from Egypt, Moses asked what he should say when the people asked what God's name was. God said to Moses, "'I am who I am.' And He said, "Thus you shall say to the children of Israel, 'I am has sent me to you'" (Exod. 3:14).

God's role in our lives is often based on our knowledge of and relationship with Him. To some, He is a doctor, lawyer, friend, deliverer, and so on. To others, He is a mother, father, sister, or brother. God can be anything to anyone based on their personal relationship, which lines up perfectly with what He says about being "I am." He is not limited; He can be anywhere, and He is all-knowing. We cannot define, measure, bind, extend, or truly conceive who He is. He can be whomever or whatever you need in your life at any time.

While God is not limited in any way, He can set limits. This is not because He is not interested in a relationship with us but because of sin. Sin is what caused Adam and Eve to be put out of the Garden of Eden, the place of abundance and often referred to as "paradise." Adam and Eve weren't just put out—they were forbidden to ever get close to Eden again. This act shows that God does not take sin lightly. Sin is a serious offense. It is the one thing that threatens our relationship with the Lord.

There Must Be Truth in the Relationship

The woman in Bethany was not trying to get to God the Father. She went after Jesus, whom she believed was truly the Son of God. This is something the religious leaders did not understand and were unwilling to learn. They were dependent on the relationship their forefathers had with God, so their approach to God was by way of tradition. They did only what their forefathers did, which was not enough to maintain a personal relationship with the Lord.

In the book of Matthew, Jesus tried to explain to the religious leaders that their rituals and practices were not enough. He told them that even though their fathers ate the manna of God that fell from heaven, their fathers were dead. If they chose to eat the bread of heaven, Jesus Christ, they would live forever (Matt. 6:58). The leaders' religion was a stumbling block that had caused spiritual blindness and the rejection of knowledge.

This same spirit of disobedience could be seen in Cain, the son of Adam and Eve. When Cain and Abel brought their offerings before God, Cain's offering was not accepted. God gave Cain the opportunity to make things right. He also informed Cain that if he refused God's command, then Cain would fall into sin. What was even more interesting was that God told Cain that he had the authority to rule over sin (Gen. 4:1-7). Remember, God has given us limited power while here on this earth because we are made in His image. This power allows us to choose for ourselves. God showed Cain he had a way out, but Cain disobeyed God just like his parents did. Cain rejected God's words and thought what he had offered was good enough.

God does not have to accept what we offer. Never kid yourself into believing that whatever you say or do is pleasing in His sight. There are things said and done in the physical houses of worship that are not pleasing to Him, but He may overlook them for a moment.

Engaging out of tradition and not out of a real relationship only limits our interaction with God. This is because the relationship lacks truth on one side. Jesus is the truth, so we know He is all-in. But we also must be all-in—that is, giving all our hearts, minds, and souls.

When Cain chose to follow his own thoughts rather than the truth set before him by God, he demonstrated the characteristics of a person who saw what he wanted to see and therefore believed what he wanted to believe. This is what happens when someone closes their mind to God and refuses to see God for who He is.

Cain shut God out. The religious leaders thought they were only shutting Jesus out, but they were also shutting God out. If we're engaging the Lord, we must do it in spirit and truth. We must seek Him on our own behalf for the purpose of a personal relationship. No two people have an identical relationship with another individual. The Lord wants truth in our relationship with Him.

I believe the woman in Bethany was sincere about going to Jesus. She believed enough to give Him her best. She acted out of truth and kindness. The Bible says God loves a cheerful giver (2 Cor. 9:7).

Are you giving God your best in your relationship or simply offering what you want to Him? It's not enough to know about God. Shift from hearing about God to actually hearing God. This benefits you because you do not have to depend on others for a word from the Lord. Your relationship is personal; it is also valuable. When you treat it that way, so will the Lord. He desires an intimate relationship with each of us.

A Living Sacrifice Was Required

Not all religious leaders avoid the truth. Some have personal relationships with the Lord and understand their submission to the Lord comes before anything else. They have chosen truth over tradition. They have chosen relationships over religion. They understand their relationships with Christ is about who He is and what He means to them. Denomination is not a factor, and neither is what their family has "always believed." It is a personal relationship built on truth and trust. These people have laid down their lives, feelings, opinions, and thoughts. They have denied themselves, taken up their crosses, and now follow Christ. They have become living sacrifices.

Jesus came and replaced what the religious leaders were accustomed to. They knew God had spoken to their fathers through the prophets. However, these prophets were men backed by the power of God. Jesus came along and shared the knowledge that He was and is the Son of God. He demonstrated His power, yet the religious leaders refused to believe. Even as Jesus was taken to the cross, He was persecuted and mocked because of unbelief. Nevertheless, His name is above every name, and today, it is through His name that we submit our prayers.

As the religious leaders chose to stick with what they knew of God through their fathers, they attempted to eliminate Jesus. This is the way of the world. When one is in a relationship with the Lord, they are no longer of the world. The only way to live representing the Kingdom of God is through Jesus Christ. The only way to do that is by having a relationship with Him. God gives us a choice between life and death (Deut. 30:15-20). Salvation is not a religion; it is not something you practice. Salvation is what we receive; it is a gift from God. God gave us the very best—Jesus Christ. And Jesus gave His very best—His life—so that you and I can live. There is no life without Christ, so there is no relationship with the Father without the Son.

The Relationship Is through Salvation

You do not need religion to receive salvation. Over the years, I have encountered many people who thought they were on their way to hell because they did not attend a traditional church. In your relationship with God, it is not where you attend worship service. Once you accept Jesus Christ as Lord and Savior, you are now a member of the Church—His Church. The Lord's Church is not made with hands; no man can physically build the Lord's Church.

Jesus is the head of His Church, which is spiritual, and He adds those of us who believe in Him to His spiritual body. We, as believers, are all over the world, yet we all belong to one body—the body of Christ, which is His Church. There is power in this relationship, and it only comes through salvation. There is no other relationship like this.

Through salvation we believe in one God and look forward to the day when we all meet Him face to face, as well as meet one another. Only God could create such a network of believers who are bound by faith, not religion. He is the only true and living God—the only true Giver of life. There is none other than God who can give us life. And for us humans, it starts with faith. Salvation comes by faith.

When Jesus died on the cross for our sins, He did not ask our permission. He voluntarily gave His life for us. His only requirement is that we believe. No other human being could so willingly die for all mankind except Jesus. Accepting Him as your Savior gives Him the opportunity to become Lord over your mind, body, soul, and spirit.

Salvation is the beginning of a new life in Christ. It is the beginning of a relationship that unveils power that you never knew. It gives you access not only to the Son of God but also to God the Father (John 14:23). Living a life backed by God can make even your biggest dreams come true (Col. 3:3). This is not religion; this is the beginning of a relationship.

Stay Focused on the Relationship

One of the hardest things about a relationship is staying focused on it. There are so many distractions. But in this relationship, Jesus wants you to make Him first. This relationship is a priority. However, surrendering to Jesus is usually where things get a bit choppy. Everyone wants the blessings of God, but not everyone necessarily wants to totally submit to His rules and His will. Keeping one's eyes on the Lord can help to lessen the fear of losing one's independence while learning to depend solely on the Lord.

When the woman in Bethany went looking for Jesus, she ran into several things that could have distracted her, including His disciples, but she kept her eyes on the goal. She was to get to Jesus no matter what happened to her. Jesus' role in this was to be right where she would need Him to be. Jesus once said, "'Ask, and it will be given to you; seek, and you will find; knock, and it will be opened to you'" (Matt. 7:7). Stay focused on Him and the relationship, and you will find the answers you need.

I believe the woman in Bethany stayed focused. She was led by the Spirit based on her own faith in Jesus. The Lord wants us to have faith to trust and follow Him. Religion is powerless without faith, but faith in Jesus can move all obstacles, including mountains.

CHAPTER FIVE

WOMAN

While Jesus was in Bethany at the house of Simon the Leper, a woman came to Him (Matt. 26:7). There was something peculiar about this woman. The Bible does not mention her name. Some say it was Mary, the sister of Martha and Lazarus. But there is no indication that the woman in Bethany was Mary. It appears she had no position or title. However, as a woman, she could have been a wife, mother, caregiver, sister, or even a servant. Nevertheless, because she was a woman, it was likely that no one cared about her name or why she was even in the house. At least, at first glance, it may have appeared that way. The fact that she was a woman was monumental.

There are a number of women in the Bible who are special in their own ways. Mary, the mother of Jesus, was chosen by God to bring Jesus Christ into the world. This caused a stir among men who questioned whether Jesus was truly God's Son. The Son of God was born of a woman? Come on! Coming on a cloud? Yes! But through a woman? That was hard for the religious leaders to accept. But let me say it again, a woman gave birth to the Son of God by way of the Holy Spirit. Yes, a woman did that.

A young woman saved the Jews when Haman persuaded King Ahasuerus to have them all destroyed. This threat to her and her people forced her to quickly become a woman of sound judgment and quick decisions. As young as she was, she walked in wisdom and ordered her people to fast for three days and nights. This woman was Esther. Esther was wise enough to know she would need more than the love of her husband the king to save her and her people from total destruction. Through prayer and fasting, along with her faith in God, Esther was able to save her people (Esther 1-10).

Then, there were the first female apostles sent by Jesus Christ to carry the good news. As they went to the tomb looking for Jesus' body, an angel told them that the Son of God had risen and that they were to go and tell His disciples to meet Jesus in Galilee (Matt. 28:5-8). As these women went on their way, they encountered Jesus and were encouraged by Him. These two women, Mary Magdalene and Mary, delivered the message that Jesus had risen from the dead to His disciples and those who would listen.

Women have been helpers according to God's plan. In the book of Genesis, God made women to be helpmates. When someone says, "I got you!" or "I've got your back!" they're saying, "I will help. I'm here for you. Don't worry." The woman in Bethany was in Simon the Leper's house to do a work. Jesus called it "a good work" (Matt. 26:10).

Her work was not viewed by the disciples as important. As a matter of fact, based on their outcries, they did not think it was necessary. But Jesus referred to her actions as "good." He did not mention worship or consider it a gift. He called it "a good work," which means that what she did took some level of effort.

The woman in Bethany did not go to Jesus with everyday perfumed oil. It wasn't even your once-in-a-year, uptown-social-event perfumed oil. The oil she used was so expensive and distinct that even the men, Jesus' disciples, noticed it just from its scent. This perfumed oil had to be something special. Instead of keeping it for herself, she gave it to Jesus in her own way. Have you ever given anything of value to Jesus that He did not have to ask you for?

An Unconceived Child Promised to God

Samuel became a prophet of God partly because his mother, Hannah, had been without child. When Hannah prayed to God for a male child, she had not yet conceived in the womb. She promised she would give the child to God for His service. Hannah conceived, and after she gave birth and weaned him, she kept her promise to the Lord. God did not ask Hannah for her son; it was all her idea (1 Sam. 1:11).

Before Hannah had ever conceived in her womb, she conceived in her mind. Her promise manifested into a great man of God, the prophet Samuel. Giving God the best we have is never wrong. He can increase, improve, and magnify anything we give Him. What if Hannah, once she had conceived and given birth, kept her son for herself? No one knows if he would have become God's prophet. Similarly, no one knows exactly how the woman in Bethany came to have such an expensive bottle of perfumed oil. We do not know how much it cost her or how long she might have had to work to purchase it, but we know it was valuable. However, in her eyes, Jesus was of greater value.

The behavior of the woman in Bethany demonstrated the character of selflessness. Too often, we keep the best for ourselves. We even keep it from the Lord. But to be honest, it has no real value until we give it over to the Lord. This may sound crazy, but the ten percent we give to the Lord has more value than the ninety percent we keep. The reason being that once ten percent is given over to the Lord, it has the backing of heaven behind it. Once the other ninety percent has been spent, it is gone. Therefore, her kindness toward Jesus with the perfumed oil went far beyond the anointing of His head. It would give her a place in history declared by our Lord and Savior, Jesus Christ (Matt. 26:13). We should freely give to the Lord what we have. He can make it go a lot further than we can.

Jesus was kind to women and treated them just as He treated anyone else. His acknowledgment of and respect toward women was different from what some of them experienced in society. He did not exclude or overlook them. When the townspeople wanted to stone a woman caught in adultery, they tried to involve Jesus. Since Jesus preached about the Kingdom of God and righteousness, they sought to get Him to accuse the woman. It was clear that the woman's gender made her guilty of sin because nothing is mentioned about the townspeople accosting the man, she had committed adultery with. In Jesus' eyes, the woman wasn't any guiltier than any of her accusers (John 8:1-11). Instead of her gender convicting her, it granted her the same grace it did the man.

I imagine there have been women who surrendered all self-indulgence, preservation, and worth when they entered the presence of the Lord. This is likely what it will be like when we see His face. We will finally realize nothing else matters. The women mentioned in the Bible did not care about what others said or thought about them. They sought the love and presence of Jesus. Maybe this was the mind of the woman in Bethany. She did not go to Jesus for accolades or praise. Nothing mattered except that she get to Jesus and do the work she was assigned to do.

Believe

The woman in Bethany and these other women had something in common: they all believed. Sometimes believing is all it takes to get us moving forward. The assignment in Bethany was made for a woman. God purposed it that way. Women were known to worship Jesus in this fashion; therefore, it would not seem so suspicious. So, her assignment was perfect for the situation at hand.

Some assignments are missed because we fail to believe right away or to believe at all. Then, of course, there are times when the assignment may appear so big that we ask God why He chose us. How could He even think to call us to such a task? This could be the reason why He sometimes disguises our assignments. He does not allow us to see the real meaning behind them until they have been completed.

While we may not always see ourselves as being strong and courageous, we are prepared for the course. When we have the mind of Christ, we can do anything God assigns us to do. If we could not, He would not even assign it. He prepares us and gives us what we need. And what He does not give us, He provides when it is needed.

Rahab, a Canaanite woman who loaned her body to men for money and perhaps other benefits, lived close to the city gate that allowed men to come and go from her home. One day, as men from the Israelites went to Rahab's home, it became obvious God had other plans for sister Rahab. She helped these men by hiding them, and she even lied to protect them. They were of God's chosen people.

By saving the lives of the men, Rahab saved herself and her own people. She eventually marry one of the Israelites and gave birth to Boaz, ancestors of King David and Jesus Christ. Rahab, a prostitute, was not even close to being called the stock of Israel, yet she is in the lineage of our Lord and Savior Jesus Christ. When God has a plan and we walk with Him in it, it works out for our good. Rahab willingly participated in God's plan, and she was blessed beyond measure.

What makes women like Hannah, Mary, Mary Magdalene, Rahab, Esther, and the woman in Bethany so courageous? We can say it is belief—belief in something or, in this case, someone greater than themselves. The Word of God gives us so much reassurance. We are reminded in Isaiah 41 that the Lord will help us; therefore, we are not to be afraid. He will give us strength and sustain us with His righteous right hand. In Him we do believe.

There Were Twelve Tribes and Twelve Princes

Too often, many of us want to know God's plan. We want to know how the plan is supposed to work and when it will be in effect. Sometimes we want to know too much. And wanting to know too much is showing a lack of trust in God.

One day, a young woman found herself in a position she had no control over. She was a maidservant, also known as a slave. She belonged to Abram and his wife, Sarai. Sarai had no children of her own, and in those days, a woman was measured by her children, so to speak. Even if their husbands were wealthy, the women desired children. Women especially wanted to have boys because their sons kept the family going in name and responsibility. But Sarai had neither a son nor a daughter (Gen. 16:1).

Childless, Sarai took matters into her own hands and gave her maidservant, Hagar, to her husband, Abram. Sarai did this so she would have children. Although Hagar would be the birth mother, she was a slave to Sarai, she really had no say in the matter. Abram laid with Hagar, and she conceived. But things did not go as Sarai planned. Because Sarai had given Hagar as a wife to Abram, Hagar received status for being the mother of her master's son. You see, God did not assign this; Sarai did. Sarai did not ask Abram what he wanted, nor did she ask Hagar what she wanted. Sarai did what Sarai wanted, and she became abusive toward Hagar, causing the maidservant to run away (Gen. 16:2-6).

Sarai did not trust God, which is why she did not wait on Him. She did things her way. Although Sarai's way did not turn out well, some magnificent things came out of her action. The angel of the Lord encouraged Hagar to return to Sarai. When the angel told Hagar about herself, she mentioned of the God who saw her, or *El Roi*. Although Hagar had been used for someone else's gain, she realized God could see her too (Gen. 16:7-14).

You may not think much of yourself because you don't believe you have much to offer.

Maybe you are overlooked while others get all of the recognition. Perhaps you don't live in the finest neighborhoods or wear the trendiest clothes. Regardless of who you are, where you are, or what you do, God sees you. You may be a woman of status, one looked upon with admiration, or you may be looked upon with disgust and filled with shame. God sees you. He does not see you with disgust, nor does He see you as the world sees you. When you see only your flaws, He sees the best you can be. When you feel like a failure, He sees you as victorious. God sees who and what you can become. Do not put your energy into what others say or believe about you. Put all of your trust in the One who made you in His image. Ask God to show you who you are to become and begin to manifest it.

It is good to be seen because this means you have God's attention. He is aware, and He cares. Sarai lacked trust, but still she was immensely blessed. Out of her womb would be birthed the twelve tribes of Israel, the chosen people of God. She was referred to by God as the mother of nations (Gen. 17:16). As a side note, I also think it's fascinating that there are twelve sets of ribs in the human body.

Sarai did not know what God had planned for her. Perhaps she felt like less than a woman when she did not have a child of her own. Maybe she felt less loved. She could have even felt useless not being able to give Abram a child when she wanted to. After all, God has given women the ability to give life. All of God's creations were able to reproduce except man. That is, until God brought forth Eve.

Many women desire to feel loved, needed, and wanted. We need to feel useful and have a place in this life. As little girls, we are mostly led to believe our biggest goal should be to get married, have children, and raise a family. This lines up with the Word of God because it is God's command to be fruitful, multiply, and fill the earth. But for the longest time, it has been the measure of success for a woman. This was the way it was back in Sarai's day, but not all women got married and raised children. Today, not all women will. But God still has a plan for each and every woman He has created. No one is left out. Yes, He has a plan for you too.

Sometimes when we can't see ahead, we try going around another way. I encourage you to wait on God. Even if you mess up, God can fix it. None of the women in the Bible were perfect. They just did things their own way. Some trusted God while others did not. But we wait on God.

When the woman in Bethany went into Simon the Leper's house to anoint Jesus, she was probably unsure of what she would encounter. But she trusted and believed that she would be accepted by Jesus. This is how we must approach God. He does not see us as less than; He sees us as His children who are capable of becoming who He created us to be.

You Were Born to Have Dominion

Sometimes it takes effort to grasp the things that God has assigned to us. Some people take hold of their assignments almost immediately while others sit and wait for the task to just suddenly get completed one day. But God has already spoken into existence that we are to have dominion. This is in whatever we choose to do or become. We are to be the best we can be. It is our faith that will help to bring our assignment into manifestation. Our part is to believe.

We must be mindful of what we have seen, heard, and discerned. Do not dismiss thoughts before considering what they mean or whether they are for the present or the future. God can use anyone to do great things just as He used the woman in Bethany. Remember, God chooses our assignments. He knows what He has prepared for us and what He has prepared us for. We must trust God and allow Him to lead the way. Surrender all and follow Him.

When we put faith and work together, amazing things can happen. However, this is most likely one of our biggest challenges. Putting the two together supports the authority to rule; the two must co-exist. Once we understand this, nothing can stop us. Had the woman in Bethany gone to Jesus afraid, His disciples chastising her might have discouraged her and caused her to run off. But she went into the house and began to operate in her assignment with authority. You, too, were born with authority. Learn to operate in it.

There Is Power in Love

God is supreme and rules with all power. His authority is not abusive. He does not neglect us. This is because His love is all-inclusive. Although His authority may have a note of conviction, love is the foundation. If He delivers a lesson through chastisement, love is the main element. God rules with the power of love. His love provides everything for mankind, and all of it is good.

To be trusted with authority is a huge responsibility that requires us to make the best decisions. Love is the most powerful gift God has given us, and I encourage you to walk in it. Speaking about love but treating people any kind of way other than with love is hypocrisy. People may not always remember what we say, but they will always remember how we treated them when they were at their best or worst.

Nothing can ever compare to the power of love displayed on the cross by our Lord and Savior Jesus Christ. Nothing will or can ever top that love. But God revealed another example of the power of His love to me. In the spirit of love, I share this with you. A woman met a man, fell in love, and eventually married him. She gave birth to their children and loved them with all her heart. She did whatever was necessary to protect her children, even teaching them the untruthful and ungodly claim that there is no God. You see, this woman was an atheist; she did not believe in God. The irony of this is that she applied the power and principles of God to her own life. How? She fell in love, then became fruitful and began to fill the earth. This woman was walking in two different mindsets because one told her to love but the other told her there was no God. Despite this, she somehow managed to find a way to love.

God loves you regardless of what you do. There is no separation between God and love because God is love (1 John 4). This power of God can exist even for those who don't believe in Him. It would be difficult for non-believers to survive without the God of love. Everyone and every living thing needs love. Even the love the non-believer displays belongs to God. Their refusal to believe or accept God does not in any way make Him less real, nor does it cause Him to cease to exist. But it makes Him all the more powerful in who He is when He becomes evident in everything and everyone around us, including in a woman who is an atheist. Little does she know, that the very God she has denied, loves her more than she could ever love her children.

The power of love can move a person to do just about anything. It can even cause them to believe they can have something their culture or belief says should not be allowed or even exist. The woman in Bethany loved Jesus in her own way. This love and her faith were enough to take her into a house where she was not welcome. Not only was she unwanted there, but her decisions were questioned by the men who were taught by Jesus Himself. Yet her faith got her in the door and sustained her. Jesus took care of the rest.

God had a plan, and it would be carried out His way, according to His will. He just needed someone who had a love for Jesus that was greater than their fears. It had to be someone who refused to be limited or restricted in any way. It required someone who could walk by faith and not be affected by what she saw or heard.

God's plan was developed with a woman in mind. Yes, a woman. This woman was not called out for not trusting in God. She was not accused of going ahead of Him. She did not ignore His promptings from the Holy Spirit, nor did she follow her flesh. She did not say the assignment cost too much, but she was acknowledged for getting the job done.

A woman walked into her God-assigned destiny. He said woman was made to be a helper, and that is exactly what this woman in Bethany did. Her assignment was not before a big crowd or on a world stage. When she walked into the house of Simon the Leper, her whole life began to change. What a mighty God we serve.

CHAPTER SIX

RESTRICTED ACCESS

Jesus was born in a barn and slept in a trough that animals ate from. He was wrapped in torn pieces of cloth known as rags. His mother, Mary, did not have cute little onesies or soft baby blankets. Jesus did not choose how He would enter this world. It was the choice of God, His Father. God planned the timing of Jesus' birth perfectly so that there would be no room for the Messiah anywhere except among the ones He came to save. Anyone who wanted access to Jesus had it, for He was literally born into the wide-open world. There was no room and board—a place for the King to lay His head. The star that signaled His birth hung high and bright in the sky, which was a representation of the light that could not be hidden. Access to Jesus was free to anyone who wanted it, yet the circumstances surrounding His birth was a sign of the rejection Jesus would face.

Jesus came to save a world that did not even know it was lost: "For unto us a Child is born; unto us a Son is given; and the government will be upon His shoulder ..." (Isa. 9:6). As an adult, Jesus entered the town of Bethany by choice. He did not choose the finer places to stay, but He went to the home of Simon the Leper. At this same time, the high priest called Caiaphas was in the palace plotting with other religious folks about how they could capture Jesus and kill Him (Matt. 26:3-5). The Lord and Savior Jesus was in the unclean, and the dirty, murderous criminals were in the clean. Talk about things appearing backwards. However, our God does not look for buildings made by hands; He looks for the temples (hearts) He makes. This way, only He can righteously determine with whom He will abide.

He's in Gated Communities and Ghettos

God said His thoughts are not our thoughts and our ways are not His ways (Isa. 55:8). He does not look for the finest neighborhoods or the largest homes; He looks at the hearts of people. So, it does not matter if Jesus is in the neighborhood of a gated community or the slums of a ghetto. He's just looking for hearts that are open to Him. Why did Jesus go into the house of Simon the Leper instead of someplace else? What was His connection with the man? The Spirit of God informed me that it did not matter if this man had been healed of his leprosy or not because, in his community, he would still be known as Simon the Leper. By choosing to go to Simon the Leper's house, Jesus set parameters to limit who would go in and out of this house while He was there.

Jesus once said to His disciples that no one could come to Him unless they were drawn in by the Father (John 6:44). At that time, Jesus was speaking of salvation. But since He was in the house of a leper, the Father would pretty much have to lead someone to the house. Before now, people had been free to follow Jesus wherever He went. The homes of those who had leprosy sometimes became infected with the disease. To the average person, this house had "condemned" written all over it. Some would have considered it a place off limits, contaminated, and possibly contagious. Just like those with leprosy, this house would have been considered unclean. A priest would usually have to go into the home and determine whether it was safe. In this case, Jesus the High Priest gave clearance for the house.

Simon the Leper's home was chosen on purpose because Jesus knew the religious folks would not enter it. Jesus knew they spoke of Him with their mouths but not with their hearts (Matt. 15:8). Clear boundaries had been set restricting access to Jesus, related to the people's fears. Few of them would have been so bold as to say what Isaiah said to the Lord: "... Here *am* I! Send me" (Isa. 6:8).

Fear Is Not in God

The Bible refers to fear as a spirit in 2 Timothy 1:7. It attacks the mind, creating thoughts that lead to certain feelings. These feelings then lead to specific behaviors. If a person thinks about something fearful, he or she may develop feelings of fear, become controlled by that fear, and eventually act out of fear. Therefore, you have to take control of fear so that it will not take control of you.

Fear did not stop the woman in Bethany from going into the house of Simon the Leper. Access or no access, this woman followed Jesus into the house. This was not a place the average human being would go into. Maybe that's it. She appeared to be average, but her purpose surely was no average assignment.

First Corinthians 1:27-29 says:

"But God has chosen the foolish things of the world to put to shame the wise, and God has chosen the weak things of the world to put to shame the things which are mighty; and the base things of the world and the things which are despised God has chosen, and the things which are not, to bring to nothing the things that are, that no flesh should glory in His presence."

God chooses those the world rejects. He can do great and mighty things through those who appear to be weak, despised, and left out.

It is interesting how God can be in the details that we want nothing to do with because we think it has nothing to do with God. Besides people not wanting to enter a leper's home, Jesus also had to deal with His disciples, who thought they knew best about what the woman in Bethany should be doing with her oil. As she began to pour her expensive oil onto Jesus' head, His disciples began to complain. It was clear the Lord had not given them access to what was taking place. However, they felt they could advise her as to how this oil could have been best used.

Someone asked why the oil was being wasted, then stated that it could have been sold for much and given to the poor (Matt. 26:7-9). When we are not mindful of the things of God, we risk being left out. Faith gives us access, but doubt can leave us standing on the other side of the door. The disciples' focus was on the natural, not the spiritual. This anointing was evidence of things to come, but they could not see it.

While others could not physically participate in the moment because of their fear, Jesus' disciples could not take part because of their lack of faith. Their lack of faith denied them the permission or freedom to understand what they were witnessing. Remember, God is not biased when it comes to selecting persons for His assignments (Rom. 2:11). The disciples ignored the fact that Jesus was the Son of the true and living God; He had come into the world to restore what was lost. They could have asked whether there was a special meaning to the anointing the woman in Bethany was performing. They could have offered their help. But they assumed they knew what her action meant. To them, it held no meaning, so they considered it wasteful.

You may have assumed you knew what God meant when He said or showed you something. We should never assume anything about God. Witnessing access to the Kingdom of heaven isn't all that common these days. We don't see everything the people of faith saw then. The Israelites witnessed the parting of the Red Sea. It was not one or two people who witnessed this; it was a nation. Those who believed and trusted in God saw things others did not. When Jesus laid hands on the sick, they were healed, delivered, and set free. People who witnessed this went and got family members, friends, and whomever else needed healing. They had access to Jesus and His healing powers.

Access to the Kingdom of heaven is what we all should want and seek. Jesus did not intend for His disciples to know and understand what was taking place when the woman in Bethany was anointing Him. If word had gotten out about the anointing He received, it could have been disastrous. So, there were few witnesses. This is similar to when Mary was informed by the angel Gabriel that she would birth Jesus the Son of God. The Bible tells of only the two of them being present. When Jesus was born, the Bible states that only Mary, His mother, and Joseph, His father, were present as others came to look on the baby Jesus.

Do not be alarmed if you find yourself alone during certain times in your life. Do not think it odd that people keep themselves away from you for what seems to be no reason. God may need to set you apart for a season, so He restricts access to you. Do not assume that you know why things are happening. Lean on the Lord and not your own understanding (Prov. 3:5-6).

The woman in Bethany went into Simon the Leper's house alone. She anointed Jesus in the natural, but her assignment was of the supernatural. Jesus' disciples, Simon the Leper and the woman in Bethany witnessed something extraordinary that night. They all had access to the King while access to the rest of the world was restricted. What a mighty God we serve.

CHAPTER SEVEN

VALUE

The disciples walked with Jesus, yet they ignored the value in Him. Supposedly they saw value in the perfumed oil. This suggests that their world wasn't that much different from ours today. In this world, many of us are taught that real value is found in material things. As in, you must be able to see or hold something for it to be valuable. This is man's doing and way of thinking. I am thankful that God saw value in us, His creation, and sent Jesus to deliver us from eternal death.

When the woman in Bethany poured the oil on Jesus, His disciples' comments can be misinterpreted as though they knew what was considered valuable. It might even have come across as if they also knew the needs of the poor. However, they did not appear to know or understand the needs of Jesus. Have you ever considered that Jesus also had needs? Jesus had feelings, fears, and needs just like us. Have you ever thought to ask Him what He wants?

Everyone has needs, and although our needs may be different, no one's needs can ever be completely met without a relationship with Christ. Jesus said, "For what profit is it to a man if he gains the whole world, and loses his own soul? Or what will a man give in exchange for his soul?" (Matt. 16:26). God is not against us having nice things, but those materials items cannot come before Jesus. There is no money, power, or material thing that can be transferred from earth to heaven or hell. In other words, whatever material things we have on earth will have no value anywhere else. A person without Christ will spend eternity in hell, where he or she has no power, reputation, or mercy. I have never heard anyone speak in the present tense about the deceased while at a funeral. It is always in the past tense because it is as if the value the person once possessed ceased to exist once they died.

Since His disciples made a quick judgment, Jesus took the opportunity to speak with them about the poor. During their complaining, the disciples went so far as to inform the woman and Jesus that the oil could have been sold and the money given to the poor (Matt. 26:9). In response, Jesus informs them that they will have the poor with them always (v. 11). I don't believe He was speaking of the financially poor only. There are people who are spiritually poor, poor in health, and people-poor. There are people who do not have a friend or loved one in the world, so they spend their birthdays and holidays alone.

Jesus' disciples' mindset would have led the poor to experience them through their deeds, instead of the people experiencing God. They did not know the real needs of the people who they claimed could benefit from the sale of the woman in Bethany's perfumed oil. Only Jesus knew their needs. The disciples viewed the anointing of Jesus as a waste because they could have used that oil for their next project. But people are not projects. We are all human beings, and we should approach others as if we are approaching Jesus.

Sometimes we hand out things others do not need or even want. Some people simply want someone to tell them things will be okay. Others need someone to tell them a testimony about making it through a rough time. And still others may want someone to listen to them. All of us want the same thing: hope. We want to know everything will be okay.

I sometimes think about people who did not qualify for some kind of support either because of their grades, lack of experience, or lack of references. It is easy to mentor someone who already has the potential to do something with their life. But try mentoring those on the streets or the ones who fail and have no one to believe in them. It would be good if we had the same love and patience for others that God has for us.

God does not pick and choose who He thinks can make it. He wants those who are struggling to stay on the path. He wants those who do not even know there is a God. He wants the ones no one wants to spend time with. Jesus said, "… 'Those who are well have no need of a physician, but those who are sick. I did not come to call *the* righteous, but sinners, to repentance'" (Mark 2:17). It's the people who have no help that really need someone in their corner.

One day while talking with Peter, one of His disciples, Jesus gave Peter a commandment. He said to Peter in three different statements, "Feed My lambs," "Tend My sheep," and "Feed My sheep" (John 21:15-17). The prerequisite was that Peter love Jesus. We cannot do anything for the people of God without having a heart for God. This becomes evident in how we treat others. If we see people through the love of Christ, then we see their value.

Jesus' disciples most likely did not mean any harm by what they said to the woman in Bethany. They wanted to act before knowing what the people they were supposedly advocating for truly needed. Only God knows the needs of His people. Jesus said to His disciples, "But seek first the kingdom of God and His righteousness, and all these things shall be added to you" (Matt. 6:33). Jesus did not want His disciples to become burdened by things, needs, and wants. He wanted them to know what was truly valuable in life, which was to go after God and His ways.

Value Is in Our Assignments

What Jesus offers is of eternal value. If we serve others with the heart of God, then the work we do can also have an everlasting effect. Whatever we do, we must do it as unto the Lord (Col. 3:23). Perhaps this is why the woman in Bethany anointed Jesus with such devotion. We must not think of our service to others as if we're checking off a box or working on another project. We must think of it as having a Kingdom effect. These may not be works seen on paper, but they are seen in heaven (1 Cor. 3:9-15). Praise God.

We are Kingdom spirits in earthly vessels who are made in the image of Almighty God. Look back at God's interaction with the first man, Adam. The Bible says God formed every beast, then brought them to Adam to see what he would call them (Gen. 2:19-20). God included Adam in the process of creation, assessed Adam's thinking and comprehension concerning His work, and engaged him in conversation by allowing Adam the liberty and authority to name every created beast. This demonstrates God's love and patience with mankind. This scene in the Garden of Eden was the first noted collaboration in a relationship between God and man. God's time, patience, and acceptance of Adam revealed He valued man and man's contributions.

Beside Jesus Christ, no other form of man's work has ever superseded God's endorsement of what Adam did when he named the beasts. A lion is still a lion. Adam also named the female gender, "woman" (Gen. 2:23). Whether Adam and Eve understood the authority given to them still remains to be known, but this is just a glimpse of the authority mankind was designed to have. It is clear to me that we were to work with God from the beginning. Even though Adam and Eve disobeyed God, He did not undo what Adam spoke when he named the animals. God saw value in Adam and Eve; He did not value one over the other. Because He saw value in the ones He made in His image, God wants to include us, male and female, in His work.

Although Jesus' disciples criticized and persecuted the woman in Bethany for her decision to anoint Jesus with the expensive oil, He saw value in His disciples. Jesus knew the day would come when their thoughts, ways, and personal goals would change. They would one day recognize the value of what Jesus did on the cross, and they would see the value Jesus saw in others. These same men would become witnesses for Christ and eventually give their lives while sharing the message of Jesus' love and sacrifice with others.

What if the woman in Bethany did not see the value in Jesus? What if she thought her best perfumed oil was too good to waste on a man who was about to die? After all, she could have waited and rubbed His deceased body with oils and spices as per tradition. What made her think or believe He was worthy of her expensive perfumed oil?

At some point in her life, maybe she was made to feel unworthy. Maybe there was a time when she wanted something or someone that was out of her reach. That is, until she met Jesus. Finally, she had met a man who defended her. Jesus did not abandon her; He validated her and her decision in a room full of men. Jesus not only defended this woman and her decision, but He expressed approval of her intentional act. This was a bold contrast to the response given to Eve, the woman who was created to be man's helper. She rejected God and His commandments. She was the woman to whom God said with disapproval, "... 'What is this you have done?'" (Gen. 3:13). She would give birth in great pain and desire the love and care of her husband. Eve brought all of that on herself and every woman after her because of her disobedience.

But God did not give up on women. He found a woman who would obey Him because she had a heart for Jesus. Her love for Him was greater than her love for herself. She understood that value was about more than cashing in; there was value in being useful. God used her to further His Kingdom. In the case of the woman in Bethany, woman would follow and not stray.

This woman in Bethany obviously believed Jesus was the Son of God. She did not yield to His disciples' criticism of her actions. She saw value in Jesus Christ. His disciples had missed the part when Jesus said they would not always have Him (v. 11). They did not question Him to learn what He was speaking about. For it would not be long before Jesus would soon shed His blood on the cross for a world of sinful people. What might have happened if God did not think we were worthy of the blood of Jesus?

Jesus once said to His disciples, "Look at the birds of the air, for they neither sow nor reap nor gather into barns; yet your heavenly Father feeds them. Are you not of more value than they?" (Matt. 6:26). Birds represent one of the smallest and helpless of God's creation, yet just like us, they are valuable to God. It was God's love that compelled Jesus to go to the cross so that we might be saved. I am grateful God sees value in each and every one of us, regardless of how small.

CHAPTER EIGHT

A GOOD WORK

Throughout life, we're evaluated in one way or another. At birth, our parents or hospital personnel count our fingers and toes. At school, our teachers evaluate our understanding of assignments given and how well we get along with others. Later in life, our spouses, neighbors, and bosses perform their own evaluations of us. Even church members critique what we say and do. Some will approve while others will not. I remember attending a home-going celebration for a person who had transitioned in life, and hearing someone say the person looked better dead than when he was alive. Even when you're dead and gone, someone will evaluate you.

As Jesus' disciples continued to persecute the woman in Bethany, calling into question her decision to anoint Him with her expensive oil, it was obvious she was getting a bit agitated. Jesus asked the question, "Why do you trouble the woman?" (Matt. 26:10). He expressed His disapproval of their behavior, which did not in any way exhibit the character of their teacher. Just as they had questioned the woman in Bethany's motives,

Jesus questioned theirs. He wanted to know why they were bothering her after He had taught them to defend and protect. They were judgmental and critical of something that, to be honest, was none of their business.

Jesus pointing out the disciples' behavior gives one comfort in knowing that He will defend those who are offended even by His own disciples. This supports what the Bible says about God not respecting any one person over another (Acts 10:34). What if Jesus had taken His disciples' side simply because they were close to Him? Sometimes, as Christians, one can behave as if God does not care about those who are not yet in the body of Christ, but this is not true. Jesus saw fit to defend the woman in Bethany, regardless of her salvation status, from the criticism of His own disciples.

With Purpose Comes Persecution

Before going to see Jesus, the woman in Bethany probably did not give much thought to the possibility of any confrontation with anyone, especially not with His disciples. After all, what was the harm in anointing Jesus with her own oil? How does one determine what is too good for one and not good enough for another? If anyone was worthy of the expensive perfumed oil, it was Jesus.

Everything Jesus did was judged by others. He hung on a cross. He bled and died for your sins and mine, yet some still think He is not good enough. Jesus came to save our souls, and persecution followed Him all the way to the cross, the grave, and back. It is clear that with purpose comes persecution. If you are truly committed to following Jesus, you will face persecution. The enemy will use whomever he can to deliver the blows.

The enemy's goal is to get you to stumble and fall in hopes that you will never get back up. So, he follows you around making all sorts of accusations. For there is one thing the enemy knows: if you fulfill your purpose, then you would have glorified God. This is because we are made in God's image. The more we begin to reflect God, the more the enemy is threatened. Therefore, he sets his sight on preventing as many people as he can from walking in their purpose. Satan fears the truth because the truth makes us free. If we are believers in Jesus Christ, then we are free (John 8:36). When we start walking in the truth, all bondage will break loose. The enemy might tighten his grip, but that's only because all his strongholds will begin to fall away.

The woman in Bethany anointing Jesus with her special perfume must have provided what looked like special treatment. His disciples were so upset. She most likely felt relieved when Jesus stepped in to defend her because it caused His disciples to back off. Jesus understood what she was going through. He had been on this earth long enough to know that persecution sometimes came from those least expected. Being quick to judge others is something we should all be aware of since we can also be judged.

The question still remains: why did the woman in Bethany anoint Jesus? Also, what did Jesus mean by a "good work"? The woman in Bethany did not say anything when the disciples asked why the waste. However, Jesus answered in a peculiar way. He said, "For in pouring this fragrant oil on My body, she did *it* for My burial" (Matt. 26:12). The keywords are "she did it for My burial." This was peculiar because Jesus appeared to voluntarily speak for her when usually others interacting with Him spoke for themselves. This included other women as well.

Perhaps the fact that this anointing was of a Kingdom purpose eluded the woman in Bethany. God will, at times, have us do things without revealing the full meaning of the tasks. He cannot risk the complete truth unfolding before its appointed time. Jesus was born to die for our sins while, at the same time, having all power and authority in heaven and on earth. He would reign as King of kings and Lord of lords, yet He did not reveal a complete explanation to His disciples until the time was right. The woman in Bethany's purpose for anointing Jesus was based on her limited knowledge of what was actually taking place. But something about this does not seem quite right. How do you anoint a person for their burial when they are still alive and well?

They Were All Alive

While His disciples had been His most visible companions, Jesus was in need of a comparable helper on the day He visited Simon the Leper. He was soon to be crucified, but there was something that needed to be done before going to the cross. And it needed to be done with as little explanation as possible. Isaiah the prophet said in Chapter 9:

> "For unto us a Child is born, unto us a Son is given; and the government will be upon His shoulder. And His name will be called Wonderful, Counselor, Mighty God, Everlasting Father, Prince of Peace. Of the increase of His government and peace *there will be* no end, upon the throne of David and over His kingdom, to order it and establish it with judgment and justice from that time forward, even forever. The zeal of the Lord of hosts will perform this."

> – vv 6-7

Isaiah was talking about Jesus. The natural man, Jesus, who was born a natural Child. Jesus was to become King, assuring David's throne would have One who would sit on it forever.

Revelation 17:14 says, "These will make war with the Lamb, and the Lamb will overcome them, for He is Lord of lords and King of kings; and those *who are* with Him *are* called, chosen, and faithful." Revelation 19:16 says, "And He has on His robe and on His thigh a name written: king of kings and lord of lords." These are just a few scriptures referring to Jesus as King of kings and Lord of lords.

Whenever God appointed a man to become king over His people, He would have Him anointed for that office. However, all those appointed by God had one thing in common: They were alive when the anointing happened. No dead man had ever become king or was anointed as king of the people. Jesus had to be alive to be anointed as king to fulfill what the prophets Isaiah, Daniel, and others said. He had to be alive to fulfill the promise God made to David. He had to be alive so that what was to be written could be true; He was Jesus of Nazareth, the King of the Jews (John 19:19).

It was not a coincidence that Pilate, a government official, wrote these words over Jesus' head. It was not a coincidence that the soldiers attempted to mock Jesus by stripping off His clothes and covering Him in a scarlet robe. They placed a crown of thorns on His head and a reed in His right hand. They did this partly because Jesus acknowledged that He was King of the Jews when Pilate questioned Him.

The army of soldiers did not know the scriptures. In Proverbs 16:9 it says, "A man's heart plans his way, but the Lord directs his steps." On the day of Jesus' crucifixion, the soldiers planned in their hearts to cause Him embarrassment, but as they knelt down on the ground and opened their mouths, they uttered, "Hail, King of the Jews." Although their motive was to mock Jesus, their words publicly acknowledged Him as King before He was crucified. The anointing had taken place in private, but God made it public.

No one knew Jesus had been anointed king except God the Father, God the Son, and God the Holy Spirit. Jesus was anointed King by a woman, and the event was unknowingly witnessed by His disciples. Then, He was verified by the governor and publicly acknowledged by the armed forces. Although Jesus was mocked by evildoers, He still received a public acknowledgment just as other kings before Him. Yes, His enemies meant it for harm, but God used it for good.

God knows the hearts of men and the fact that men like to follow tradition. During the Old Testament times, it was common for kings, priests, and others to be anointed by other men. So, it was expected that if Jesus was to become King, He would most certainly be anointed by a man. However, if this had happened, the people would have immediately known He was King. Therefore, God took a different approach. Very few men, if any, would believe God would use a woman to anoint His Son as King. After all, God had created man first. Anointing was a man's job. What could possibly qualify a woman to anoint a man, especially Jesus? No one was going to believe that. It was too far-fetched to even consider.

Unconventional Ways

In order for the anointing of Jesus to take place, two things had to happen. First, people had to be kept away from Jesus. This is what led to Jesus being in the home of Simon the Leper. The people's own fears about entering the home of a leper kept them away and restricted access to Jesus. Second, God had to get someone to anoint Jesus without anyone being the wiser. It would have to be someone that no one would ever suspect. It would have to be a woman—the woman in Bethany—with her expensive fragrant oil.

God, in His wisdom and creativity, used a woman without ever mentioning it to anyone. And it worked. This suggests that we should not count on God doing things the exact same way. But we can count on the fact that our God is always faithful.

God does things in some of the most unconventional ways. He said, "'For My thoughts *are* not your thoughts, nor *are* your ways My ways ... For *as* the heavens are higher than the earth, so are My ways higher than your ways, and My thoughts than your thoughts'" (Isa. 55:8-9). God uses those who are despised and made to believe they are inferior and unwanted. Could it be possible God also chose to use a woman to anoint Jesus because of those who had already sought to make Him their king? When Jesus fed the five thousand, the men believed Jesus was the prophet who was to come (Deut. 18:15-16); therefore, they sought to make Him their king (John 6:4-15). To avoid being forced into something by these men, Jesus had to get away. Although the men were on to something, it was not their call to make. These men were only looking out for themselves.

Jesus would become King, but He had to appear on the cross first. There was no way people would have allowed their newly anointed King to be crucified. There would have been a war. All prophecy concerning Jesus had to be fulfilled both spiritually and naturally. Some believed David's kingdom to come was of a spiritual state, but David was also a natural man. His kingdom here on earth was also in a natural state. I do not believe God would fulfill one and not the other. God does not rest until His work is finished.

Although Jesus had not yet made it to the cross, He was willing to do—without question—whatever the Father asked of Him. Jesus knew what the Father expected of Him, and He purposed in His heart to do the Father's will. There was a time when John the Baptist tried to persuade Jesus to baptize him, but Jesus refused because they had to fulfill all righteousness (John 3:14-15). Regardless of what He wanted to do, Jesus knew He had to do what the Father wanted. As Jesus allowed the woman in Bethany to anoint Him, He knew He would not be in the grave long enough to cause a stench. He had to be about His father's business to wake up the dead and set prisoners in hell free.

The Work of the Father Increases Outcomes

Because Jesus needed to be anointed before going to the cross, God used the woman in Bethany who desired to anoint Jesus for His burial. God's thoughts and the woman's thoughts were different; however, the work performed by the woman in Bethany produced both outcomes. A lesson in this is that we should not question God, but we should simply do as He says because our understanding of the Kingdom is limited. Our sight is limited.

Our hearing is limited. Our best response is to go where He says go and do what He says do. That was what the woman in Bethany did. She did what she was led to do.

Jesus was protective of the woman in Bethany while she was in His presence. He knew and understood the work of His Father well. If it had been revealed that God had sent a woman to anoint His Son as King, it could have gotten really ugly for Jesus and the woman in Bethany. When God created everything, He looked over all His work and saw that it was good. He did not need anyone else to approve or validate Him and what He did.

After all these years, all God created remains just as He determined. It was all good then, and it is all good now. So, just like His Father, Jesus acknowledged a good work. He called it a good work because He knew it was of the work of His Father. Jesus had not referred to anyone else's work as being good before nor since.

Jesus' anointing as King also had to happen through a woman to fulfill God's Word regarding the seed of the woman and seed of the serpent. On the day when God spoke to the serpent, He said, "'And I will put enmity between you and the woman, and between your seed and her Seed; He shall bruise your head, and you shall bruise His heel" (Gen. 3:15). God made it clear that this would be between the woman and the enemy. Even as God spoke of the seed, He referred to Him as the woman's seed. This may be due to the enemy tricking Eve to eat of the forbidden fruit first, as well as the Son of God coming through a woman, the Virgin Mary. Nevertheless, the woman and the enemy would oppose one another, and her seed would rise high above his. When we surrender all to God—loving, trusting, and obeying Him—we find that He works in mysterious, unconventional ways. This truly was a good work.

While There Is Purpose, There Is Also Praise

Jesus did not call the woman in Bethany good. He said she had done a good work. It was obvious that this woman had a heart for Jesus. Her work left a good impression on Him. Because Jesus voiced approval, we can conclude that her action met His standards and was highly effective.

One day, we will stand before God and receive judgment, whether good or bad, regarding what we did on this earth. Jesus acknowledging the woman in Bethany's work as good in front of His disciples immediately catapulted her into a light no other woman had ever experienced. While other women followed Jesus and assisted Him out of their own resources, Jesus had not spoken publicly about any other woman in this way before. Unlike Eve, the woman in Bethany was not chastised for being disobedient; she was praised for doing a good work.

Jesus did not stop at acknowledging the woman in Bethany. His words helped to show His disciples that women can work for Him and His Kingdom, and He welcomed it. The disciples got to see Jesus interact with a woman on a level they had not seen before. Through Jesus' words, the woman in Bethany's work received a place in history; her work was validated. He did not say she would become known in the neighborhood church or the state association. He said, "'Assuredly, I say to you, wherever this gospel is preached in the whole world, what this woman has done will also be told as a memorial to her'" (Matt. 26:13). What this woman did was worthy of worldwide acclaim; it was to be remembered.

What she did was good in the sense that it was morally right because she was obedient to complete the work that was needed. It was good in that it was profitable because it had the approval of Jesus and was declared a good work. And it was good in that it was fruitful; it was added to the gospel of Jesus Christ and would be preached all over the world.

Jesus purposely chose to exalt the work of the woman in Bethany in front of His disciples. This was clearly the way of God. His actions cast a light on the negative ways women were treated due to tradition and religious boundaries. Women were needed to help advance the Kingdom of God, and they were capable of doing so.

God demonstrated how He could use women according to His purpose. Being born female is a good thing. The female role is as valuable in the Kingdom of God as ever before. God created a space especially for us.

God has always had a way of shaking things up. When He comes through, there is bound to be an earthquake. While the ground did not physically shake when the woman in Bethany anointed Jesus, the event shook up the disciples. It got their attention. Little did the disciples know that things would be shaken up even more when Jesus got to the cross. When Mary and the women would go to the tomb to retrieve His body, again God would move the earth.

CHAPTER NINE

FAITH

*L*abels have a way of identifying what others may not immediately notice. Bartimaeus, like Simon the Leper, was labeled "blind" in the book of Mark. Jesus was even labeled "Jesus of Nazareth" to identify the small town He came from. Nazareth was not known for anything much except for Jesus Christ who had once lived there. Had it not been for His mother Mary, Nazareth might not have ever been mentioned.

Imagine how you might feel if people labeled you based on your past or even your present condition. Suppose people referred to Rahab as her past identity everywhere she went. This is enough to take a toll on any human being. But people like Simon, Rahab, and Bartimaeus demonstrated they were people of faith. They survived in a world that projected an image of them as being less than everyone else.

When others measure you according to their standards, they attempt to leave the impression with you that their perceptions are correct. Therefore, things must be the way they see them. But God said, "'For My thoughts are not your thoughts, nor are your ways

My ways'" (Isa. 55:8). God meant this for everyone, including those who think their ways are best. Our duty is to put our faith in God, not the ideas or opinions of man.

As Jesus taught in the synagogue, those present were offended by His teachings. They asked, "'Is this not the carpenter's son?'" (Matt. 13:55). They didn't think much of Jesus' father Joseph, so they questioned Jesus' authority in speaking with knowledge. Who did He think He was? This is another trick of the enemy. Satan would rather we put one another down. Knowing who you are is a dangerous thing in Satan's kingdom. Even he knows you are someone special in the eyes of God. You are a child of the King.

Jesus operated by faith. He knew who He was. At the age of twelve, He traveled with His mother Mary and His father Joseph. After searching for Jesus for about three days, they found Him in the temple sitting and talking with the teachers (Luke 2:41-52). When Mary shared with Him how they had been anxiously looking for Him, Jesus answered, "'Why did you seek Me? Did you not know that I must be about My Father's business?'" (Luke 2:49).

Jesus did not discuss with Mary and Joseph the fact that He knew who He truly was. He just began walking in who He was. Once He knew and understood who He was, He believed it and began to operate in it. This is what faith looks like. You don't need permission from others to be who you are. Be who you know God created you to be. Walk in it and be the best you can be at it.

Just like Jesus, the disciples were labeled and mistreated. Some people even made fun of them, saying they were drunk (Acts 2:13). This, however, was not true. They were filled with the Holy Spirit. While the disciples did not come from the best neighborhoods, have the best education, or have loads of money, they became known as men who turned the world upside-down (Acts 17). No other men would ever go on to do what these men did. Why not? Because their faith, along with being filled with the Holy Spirit, allowed them to do things others could not.

Before getting to the point of having such faith, the disciples had some things to learn. The enemy used all of his tricks to distract them. If mankind ever set his mind to truly walk in the authority given to him by God, the enemy could not stop him. The mind is a powerful tool when it is properly prepared with a foundation such as faith. This is something Jesus knew and His disciples would one day figure out.

When the disciples were hostile toward the woman in Bethany for pouring the perfumed oil on Jesus, they appeared to lack faith at that time. Their thinking was not of the things of God but of the minds of worldly men (Matt. 16:23). They called this woman wasteful, which challenged her thinking. But what happened to the faith they had in Jesus and who He was? They had been sitting under His teachings and learning from Him for three years. How did they become so easily distracted by what the woman in Bethany did?

You Cannot Do Kingdom Work with a Worldly Mind

If the woman in Bethany had proceeded with a worldly mind, she probably would not have ever gone looking for Jesus. She would have thought the way His disciples did: her oil was too valuable to waste. Jesus' disciples were lacking the one thing He had demonstrated over and over again: faith. Everything Jesus did was of faith, love, and hope. All the money in the world would never be enough, which is why it is always needed and always being raised. But faith can move problems completely out of your way regardless of what others say or think the solution is. Faith in our God is the key to solving our problems.

One day, when Jesus first told the disciples about His impending crucifixion, Peter declared it would not happen and began to rebuke the Son of God. Jesus then rebuked the enemy that was using Peter (Matt. 16:23). Jesus had to get Peter and the others to see there was no way they would be successful for the Kingdom of God if they were going to think like worldly men. This was not a natural enemy, so it could not be defeated with natural remedies. The Bible says, "For we do not wrestle against flesh and blood, but against principalities, against powers, against the rulers of the darkness of this age, against spiritual *hosts* of the wickedness in the heavenly *places*" (Eph. 6:12). It has to be Power to power. This Power can only come from the Lord, and it requires faith.

Just as with His former disciples, Jesus is not surprised at our lack of faith. Imagine the things we could do if we believed and didn't doubt. Jesus said to a father, "If you can believe, all things *are* possible to him who believes" (Mark 9:23). Jesus did not say *some* things are possible. He said *all* things are possible. Faith removes limitations. Where fear and doubt bind and restrict, faith sets free. Any human being can do great things if he or she only has faith.

Jesus used the word "can" when He spoke with the father in Mark 9:23 because He wanted the father to exercise his faith right then and there. This dad did not have to go off anywhere to pray. If he wanted to, he could have given himself permission to believe in Jesus and set his son free at that moment. This is a good example of living in the present. Too often, we worry about things that are not yet present but might happen. Do not worry about what might happen. Trust in the Lord. If it helps, break your situations down moment by moment so as to have enough faith for one moment at a time. Thank God for each moment and rest in His presence. You might be surprised at what the Lord can do in a moment of faith.

I believe the woman in Bethany rested in God. She went to Jesus in a moment of faith. If she had thought about how the disciples might have treated her, she might not have gone in and anointed Him. But she took things moment by moment. She had to first get in the house before she could do the assignment. Take first things first, then move on to the next.

Faith Is Your Responsibility

The responsibility to believe is on us. The good thing is that all things are possible to those who believe. It should not hinder you if your spouse does not believe. Your neighbors' disbelief should not affect your belief because it is a personal response for everyone. Faith does not happen because someone else believes. Faith is based on what you, the individual, believe.

Faith is not about size. Faith is about pleasing God. When we operate by faith, we reflect the image of God. Faith causes us to look more and more like His children. When Jesus spoke to His disciples about having faith the size of a mustard seed, He was showing that the smallest amount of pure faith could defeat the largest problem (Matt. 17:20). In other words, it's not the size of our faith; it's the realness and sincerity of it. When the disciples were filled with the Holy Spirit, it was as if their faith became potent because nothing could stop them from doing the things of God.

Displaying the tiniest bit of faith pleases God so much that He is willing to move on our behalf. He showed us this by sending Jesus Christ to the cross and allowing Him to die so that we, who believe, could live. We are saved by faith. To believe a man named Jesus died for my sins requires faith. To believe He is still alive requires faith. One day, because of that faith, I had an encounter with the Lord. Keep believing. What you believe can manifest before your eyes.

God the Father seeks those who will worship Him in spirit and truth (John 4:23). This requires faith. Regardless of your situation, to get into His presence, you must believe that He is who He says He is. Proverbs 9:10 says, "The fear of the Lord is the beginning of wisdom, and the knowledge of the Holy One is understanding." Fear means we are to respect God. However, people do not generally respect what they do not know or understand. This is no fault of God's for He said, "My people are destroyed for lack of knowledge" (Hos. 4:6). At this time, the relationship that was to be had between man and God was hindered by other men. The relationship was either broken or nonexistent. Faith can get you to that relationship.

Faith in Jesus Christ is our way to the Father. He is the key to restoration of those broken relationships. Trusting in Him can get you to a place where worship is wholly fulfilled according to the Lord's requirements. Jesus said it this way, "'You shall love the Lord your God with all your heart, with all your soul, and with all your mind'" (Matt. 22:37). We must keep this commandment in order to worship God in spirit and truth. We can begin through faith.

When we believe God is who He says He is, He will do what He says He will do. If you want your life to please God, live by faith. With faith, your life can be everything you want it to be and more. It is possible, if you will believe.

Faith Is Manifested by What Is Spoken and Heard

When God spoke, His words literally came to life. The heavens and the earth responded to what they heard: "So then faith *comes* by hearing, and hearing by the Word of God" (Rom. 10:17). Faith gives us access, through Jesus the Son, to God the Father. Faith is what pleases our heavenly Father because it demonstrates our trust in Him. Our show of faith is an acknowledgment of who He is. Our faith reflects His image which, in essence, is who we are. Imagine being the true reflection of who He is in all that we say and do. Just as God displayed power through His words, there is power in our very own tongues. Whatever we speak, whether good or bad, can manifest. The words we speak can create our own little worlds around us. Speak what you believe is possible; sow seeds of faith and watch your words come to life. Anything is possible to those who believe.

Jesus has given us a way out of thinking we must possess an abundance of faith. He said, "... 'For assuredly, I say to you, if you have faith as a mustard seed, you will say to this mountain, "Move from here to there," and it will move; and nothing will be impossible for you'" (Matt. 17:20). The idea that faith the size of a small seed can move a mountain is astounding. Jesus using such an analogy supports the fact that the Kingdom of God is a powerful entity. Faith, regardless of its size, produces sustainable results because it is of God. The light, our God spoke into existence in the beginning, is still shining bright today (Gen. 1:3).

When Jesus walked on the earth, blessings seemed to follow Him, flowing from Him to others. This was the evidence of what He walked in: faith. Faith does not come by title, position, lineage, money, or education. It is given by God. He has placed this power inside us, regardless of how we use it. We cannot see words, but we can see the results of them.

Faith Is the Key

One day when Jesus was talking with His disciples, Peter, speaking by faith, announced that Jesus was the Christ, the Son of the living God (Matt. 16:16). Peter did not know this of his own accord. Jesus said, "'Blessed are you, Simon Bar-Jonah, for flesh and blood has not revealed *this* to you, but My Father who is in heaven'" (Matt. 16:17). By faith, Peter had accessed the Kingdom of heaven. Faith is the key to the Kingdom of God.

While not everyone may have houses, cars, and land, anyone can have faith. Faith is one of the most valuable assets available to mankind. God makes it available to everyone who believes. It is up to you as an individual as to how you choose to use your faith. Many people have been healed by faith. Some have been delivered from bondage by their faith. And others, through hard work and faith, have walked into their destinies.

Faith is the key to life-changing events. By faith, I am saved. Have I ever seen the Lord? No, not face-to-face, but I have felt His presence. I know that He is real, and my faith increases interactions with Him all the more (John 14:23). Worldly possessions, and personal successes will not do. What you need is faith.

God, in His amazing way, made faith a resource to man that is capable of producing both tangible and intangible results. This is one of the reasons the gospel of Jesus Christ is so important; there is no other way to acquire faith. The Word of God produces faith, and that faith produces Kingdom results.

I am reminded of how two disciples went to follow Jesus after having followed John the Baptist. One day when they were out, John the Baptist saw Jesus. When he said, "Behold the Lamb of God," two of John's disciples left him and began following Jesus (John 1:36). Although Jesus had not said one word to the disciples, they turned and began following Him based on what they heard John the Baptist say. They believed what they heard about Jesus, the Lamb of God.

Faith is the one and only thing that can lead to salvation. Jesus said, "'I am the way, the truth, and the life. No one comes to the Father except through Me'" (John 14:6). Before one can be saved, she has to believe that Jesus is the Son of God. Faith in who He is is the answer to the problems in this world. It is the key to healing those of sicknesses and diseases. It is the key to restoring broken homes and marriages. Faith can open doors where there are no doors. Faith will tell you that you can when everyone else says you cannot. Faith in Jesus Christ is truly the beginning of life.

As the woman in Bethany found her way to Jesus, little did she know that the faith she walked in would change her life. All she took with her was a bottle of expensive perfumed oil and hopes of getting to see Jesus. She was not known as anyone special, but she had faith. Sometimes life requires letting go of what we know and taking hold of faith. Having faith does not mean she wasn't afraid, but it means her faith gave her the confidence she needed to face whatever came her way. This is what makes faith so valuable. No matter how hard or dark the beginning may be, the end result will make it all worth it because it was done by faith.

Faith got the woman in Bethany into the presence of Jesus, and it got her through the assignment that was given to her. Faith gave her an opportunity that no other person was given. God loves it when we put our trust in Him because He gets to show us who He is and who we can become by faith.

CHAPTER TEN

THE ANOINTING — NOTHING WASTED

Jesus did not reveal the complete story about His anointing to His disciples when the woman in Bethany anointed Him. It was not the right time. However, when Pilate, the governor, asked Jesus if He was a king, Jesus answered, "… 'You say *rightly* that I am a king …'" (John 18:37). It was the right time. Pilate did not attempt to question Jesus' authority. Instead, he went to the people and said to them, "'… Do you therefore want me to release to you the King of the Jews?" (v. 39). The woman in Bethany anointed Him, but it was Pilate who revealed Jesus as King.

While His disciples may not have understood the reason behind Jesus' anointing, they were wrong about the expensive perfumed oil. It was not wasted (Matt. 26:7-8). It did just what God intended. Every work that Jesus ever did, or that was done for Him, had purpose. Nothing was ever wasted but was useful for the glory of God. We can see this in different stages of Jesus' life.

Being that He is the Son of God, Jesus could have entered this world as an adult male. However, He came by way of a natural birth—as a newborn representing mankind in the most natural form. He experienced each stage of life until adulthood. His level of communication was astoundingly appropriate when engaging others, no matter His age or theirs. At the age of twelve, He stayed behind in Jerusalem and was found sitting with the teachers in the temple listening to them and asking questions (Luke 2:41-50). While His mother and father were upset once they found Him, Jesus gained favor with men and with God (v. 52).

Another time when His disciples tried to turn some children away who were brought to Him, Jesus replied that the children be allowed to come to Him (Matt. 19:13-15). He had been a child, so he knew what it was like to be overlooked, dismissed, and ignored. He engaged these children as He had adults. He ministered to them by laying His hands on them, and He commented that "of such is the kingdom of heaven" (Matt. 19:6), meaning that heaven belonged to those who were like children (humble, loving, kind, and forgiving). He used the characteristics of children to teach His disciples a lesson. Nothing was wasted.

Jesus humbled Himself as He went to John the Baptist to be baptized (Matt. 3:13). He faced the unwarranted persecutions of others talking about Him and calling Him a sinner although He had done nothing wrong. Jesus humbled Himself in every way possible before God and man, drawing those who might have walked away because of the shame of their sins. He knew the stigma of sin, yet He joined in with those who repented and was baptized. His actions were not for show. They showed the human side of Jesus and helped to strengthen others. His humility led to the Holy Spirit, in the form of a dove, resting on Him and God the Father acknowledging Jesus as His Son. God expressed how pleased He was with Jesus in front of the witnesses present (vv 13-17). His humble act of obedience was not wasted.

As His disciples knew Him, Jesus had never wasted anything. To them, what the woman in Bethany did appeared to be an outright careless use of a valuable resource. And what made it even harder for them to accept was that Jesus did not refuse the woman's extraordinary act. He seemed to welcome it. His disciples had never seen Jesus act the way He did before.

When Jesus fed more than five thousand people with two fish and five loaves of bread, He had His disciples take up twelve baskets full of leftovers (Matt. 14:16-21). Then, there was the time when He had them take up seven baskets full after feeding another crowd of more than four thousand (Matt. 15:36-38). Nothing was wasted. So, it was unlike Jesus to allow a woman to pour expensive oil on Him for what appeared to be no good reason.

When Aaron and his sons were to be anointed, God gave Moses specific instructions to make a "holy anointing oil." This oil was so holy that God told Moses no other oil was to ever be made like it. The oil would be used to anoint the tabernacle of meeting, the Ark of the Covenant, and the articles, as well as to anoint Aaron and his sons for consecration. This oil was beyond special; it was used to set the people and things that belonged to God apart from everyone and everything else. It was a holy anointing oil throughout Moses' generation (Exod. 30).

Jesus was filled with the Holy Spirit when He was led into the wilderness by the Spirit (Luke 4:1). He was the Messiah, the anointed One. The anointing performed by the woman in Bethany was symbolic for the sake of the promises made by God. Therefore, Jesus was anointed both in the natural and spiritual realms. The natural man had to be fully represented regarding His purpose for coming to earth. Yes, Jesus would die for all our sins, but He would become King first. God promised David that his seed and throne would endure forever (Ps. 89:34-37). Jesus would have authority over heaven and earth. Unlike other kings before Him, Jesus did not send His people into battle. He went in and fought for us. As Jesus was lifted up on the cross, He began governing. First, He pardoned the criminal who hung beside Him, asking Jesus to remember him. Pardoning this criminal of his sin was something only the King of kings could do. Then, Jesus gave that criminal the right to salvation and to fellowship with Him in His Kingdom, as only the Savior could. Jesus took full responsibility for all the people, asking the Father to forgive them for they did not know what they were doing (Luke 23).

His ruling as King began and became evident on the cross. As Jesus hung there, He relinquished His natural bond with His mother Mary, delegating her care to a trusted disciple. Knowing that His work was done and believing God the Father was pleased, He then gave up His earthly life (John 19:25-30). No other human being could have done what Jesus did. Nothing was wasted.

After His resurrection, Jesus said to His disciples, "All authority has been given to Me in heaven and on earth" (Matt. 28:18). Remember, this authority was not displayed only to His apostles at the time but also to others to come, including Saul who became Apostle Paul. Saul was one of the first to hear Jesus speak out of heaven when man was used to hearing God the Father speak from heaven (Acts 9:1-6). Jesus' ruling in heaven and on earth was displayed for the natural man to see—in particular, those like Saul who probably would not have ever believed it had he not heard and seen it for himself. Nothing was wasted.

As powerful as this revelation is, none of it was easy. God had prepared for the day of Jesus' top-secret anointing because Satan sought a more opportune time to tempt and oppose Jesus (Luke 3:12-13). He did not want Jesus to go to the cross as the King. Remember, when they were in the wilderness, Satan tried all he could to get Jesus to reveal He was the Son of God. At the same time, Satan tried to coax Jesus into believing that he had the authority to offer Jesus the kingdoms of the world (Matt. 4:3-10). He wanted Jesus to serve him; he never wanted Jesus to become known to man as the Son of God because Jesus was man's only way back to God. I thank God for His Son who so willingly gave His life for someone like me. He spared nothing, not even His life, to save you and me.

If we want to do a good work for the Kingdom of God, we have to forget life as we know it. We cannot rely just on natural instincts, meaning the flesh; we must rely on God and His Spirit. Everything you have been through has had a purpose. Nothing has been or ever will be wasted.

One day, as His disciples were watching Jesus, they asked, "'Who can this be, that even the winds and the sea obey Him?'" (Matt. 8:27). They had never seen anyone like Him before. I believe this is partly because Jesus lived beyond the flesh. Yes, He was made of flesh, but He did not operate solely in the flesh. He operated in His first birthright, the spirit. While on earth, Jesus showed us that life was more than a natural experience. Real life is of the spirit. Man did not even come alive until God breathed His Spirit into him. It was then that we became living souls (Gen. 2:7). We just happen to be in a natural setting.

If you have spent the first part of your life doing everything according to the flesh, none of it is wasted. It is not too late to begin living according to the spirit as Jesus did. If you have given your life to Jesus Christ, then allow Him to take control. He will operate through you by way of the Holy Spirit. Therefore, bringing forth those good works you are destined to perform.

When God the Father created the heavens, the earth, and everything in them, He said His creation was good. Everything was formed by way of His mouth through spoken words, and all of it was good. I believe this means God's plans for heaven, earth, and man have always been for good. Everything was meant to be good and bring about more good.

The woman in Bethany was given something good, and she did not waste it. She used it to provide a needed service to the Lord. And because of this, she was acknowledged for doing a good work. The Bible says,

> "For whom He foreknew, He also predestined *to be* conformed to the image of His Son, that He might be the firstborn among many brethren. Moreover whom He predestined, these He also called; whom He called, these He also justified; and whom He justified, these He also glorified."

> – Rom. 8:29-30

The woman in Bethany could have used her expensive perfumed oil for anything she wanted; it was her choice. However, God knew she would use the oil on Jesus. This was a part of her calling. God knows each and every one of us. He knows who will do His will, for He has already chosen us to do so. Each of us who are chosen and called by God have something we can use to glorify God—the words we speak, the songs we sing, the way we treat one another, as well as the way we share the gifts He has given to us. There are many ways we can reflect the image of God to others. Hopefully, when we stand before the Lord one day, we will hear Him say, "Well done. You have done a good work."

PART 2

POSITIVE, THOUGHT-PROVOKING DISCUSSIONS

A GOOD WORK

DISCUSSIONS

Discussions can be done in groups or alone, allowing for deeper reflection. The goal is to be honest, learn, and grow in all the ways God would have you. You will find that not all thought-provoking questions are necessarily about the characters mentioned in the book. Some questions are designed to encourage you to reflect on how you might respond or view things in a given situation. These discussion questions aim to encourage and support you in becoming even greater than you already are. God expects a good work from me and from you.

Discussions 1-10

Discussion 1: Under Development

Discussion 2: Relatable and Relevant

Discussion 3: Be Mindful

Discussion 4: Religion but No Relation

Discussion 5: Woman

Discussion 6: Restricted Access

DISCUSSION 1
UNDER DEVELOPMENT

Definition: Not normally or appropriately developed; possessing a relatively low economic level of industrial production and standard of living

The day Adam and Eve sinned, man began overdeveloping in the flesh and regressing in the spirit. God said to Adam, "'In the sweat of your face you shall eat bread till you return to the ground, for out of it you were taken; for dust you are, and to dust you shall return'" (Gen. 3:19).

The human race is the only creation made in the image of God that is underdeveloped. There is an abundance materially, but much is lacking spiritually. Human beings have taken to watching one another instead of watching God. Few are running for the real prize (Phil. 3:14). Most eyes are on economics, trying to get as much as they can get.

Does this sound familiar to you? Eve's focus was self-centered. Instead of keeping her eyes on the Lord, she ended up talking with a serpent. She was made to communicate with man and God. She was to rule over serpents. Did you catch that? Woman was supposed to rule over the enemy. Now all of mankind has to pray, asking God for help to keep the enemy away.

The question generally asked is, how did Eve stray from Adam? I wonder, *how did Adam and Eve stray from God?* They most likely strayed just like any of us have in the past. When we take our eyes off the Lord, thinking we are big enough to stand on our own, we are bound to fall.

Adam and Eve fell as soon as they walked off on their own. They left God and His commandment behind, and their underdeveloped minds turned to the enemy and what they could gain from eating the fruit. This is just like a toddler learning to walk. Regardless of how much we try to keep them from falling, they usually get away from us when the inevitable happens. They have yet to realize that they need the ability to balance. Until then, Mommy and Daddy are there to help them walk—just as the Lord wants to help us walk in His ways.

Made in His Image

Being made in the image of God should give us immediate knowledge that He is the one we are to follow. Little kids try to imitate their parents because they are the ones the children see the most. When they start spending time with other little kids, they may pick up some habits, but children tend to stick closer to what they see at home. This distinguishes the relationships.

If you do not have a meaningful relationship with the Lord, you will follow what you know. Whether TV, magazines, your own mind, or people you associate with, you will follow someone or something. Maybe this is part of man's problem. But we must be developed in the Spirit by God.

So, how does one stay in a relationship with the Lord being that He is invisible? Again, this is just like little children. As soon as Mom or Dad is out of sight, the kid wanders off. Just because they cannot physically see Mom or Dad does not mean Mom or Dad cannot see them. As a parent, we can call our child's name, and even if they cannot see us, they know our voice. This is due to the relationship we have formed with them. They know our voice; you know your parent's voice.

God is only invisible to our eyes with the exception of the beautiful creation we see around us and the people who walk so carefully in His Spirit. God is visible if you know where to look for Him. And He can be heard if you know how to listen for Him.

Studying the Bible is one way to stay in relationship with the Lord. The Bible teaches us how God interacts with His creation, and it teaches us how we are to interact with Him and one another. The key is that we must apply what we learn. Application is a process. It can be trial after trial before one walks the way they desire with God, but do not focus on the process. Focus on the outcome—the prize. Get to the outcome, then you can go back and look at where God has brought you from.

The Apostle Paul put it this way: "I press toward the goal for the prize of the upward call of God in Christ Jesus" (Phil. 3:14). Keep your eyes on the prize. Know that God will never lead you wrong. This relationship is for a lifetime, and He will always lead you in the paths of righteousness because it is His name that is on the line (Ps. 23:3). Always keep your eyes on Him. You cannot go wrong by following Him.

Adam and Eve paid a price for their disobedience, and it affected all of mankind. While we are to help one another, each one of us is also responsible for our individual relationships with the Lord. Assessing our own development and growth is one way of being responsible and holding ourselves accountable for our own actions. This, of course, starts with accepting Jesus Christ as your Lord and Savior. This is the beginning of a relationship with the Lord. As you abide in Him, and He in you, then comes the growth.

Genesis 1–3; Matthew 26:1–13; John 14; Hebrews 12:5-6

Discussion

Love, Accountability, and Responsibility

Love

1. When she disobeyed God's command by eating off the tree and giving some to her husband, Eve made a personal decision that placed her in a position to be chastised by a loving God and abandoned by an angry man. Do you think Eve gave any thought to what she was doing? Explain your answer.

2. What do you think could have been going through Eve's mind when she felt the disappointment of Adam and God?

_____

_____

_____

_____

_____

_____

_____

_____

_____

_____

3. When God is displeased with you, is that reason to question His love for you? Read Hebrews 12:5-6. Explain your answer.

_____

_____

_____

_____

_____

_____

_____

_____

_____

_____

4. Have you ever told the Lord you love Him? What is it you believe the Lord expects from you? Read John 14:15. Explain your answer.

_____

_____

_____

_____

_____

_____

_____

_____

_____

_____

_____

5. Eve chose to blame the serpent when confronted about her sin. What are other things you could say to express your heart to God? What did Daniel do in Daniel 9:4-5?

_____

_____

_____

_____

_____

_____

_____

_____

_____

_____

_____

6. Love is more than words. Love has to be displayed in your responses, words, actions, and motives. Write your plan for loving the Lord with all your heart, mind, soul, and strength.

_____

_____

_____

_____

_____

_____

_____

_____

_____

_____

7. What, if anything, stood out to you about God's love for Eve? What about His love for the woman in Bethany?

_____

_____

_____

_____

_____

_____

_____

_____

_____

_____

_____

_____

_____

_____

_____

_____

_____

_____

_____

While both of these women interacted with God, whether it was the Father or the Son, their individual decisions set them apart. Eve disobeyed God, even leading her husband Adam to go along. The woman in Bethany did what she could to help Jesus.

While Eve was chastised by God, the woman in Bethany was persecuted by Jesus' disciples. God used the results of Eve's disobedience to set things in place for Jesus to one day go to the cross not only for Eve's sin but for all sin. Jesus praised the woman in Bethany for her good work. God loved them both. The Bible says, "... 'Love will cover a multitude of sins'" (1 Pet. 4:8).

8. Share your thoughts on how you perceive each woman was treated. Were the scenarios justified in your opinion? Explain your answer.

_____

_____

_____

_____

_____

_____

_____

_____

_____

_____

_____

9. How confident are you in knowing God loves you, and how did you get to this place of assurance?

_____

_____

_____

_____

_____

_____

_____

_____

_____

_____

10. The love God has for His people is a never-ending love. This is why He sent His Son, Jesus, to die for your sins. Have you acknowledged that love by accepting Jesus Christ as your Lord and Savior? Explain your answer.

_____

_____

_____

_____

_____

_____

_____

_____

_____

_____

11. Jesus said to love others as yourself (Matt. 22:39). How are you to love yourself? What are the examples given in Proverbs 19:8, John 15:9, and Ephesians 5:29?

_____

_____

_____

_____

_____

_____

_____

_____

_____

_____

_____

_____

Proverbs 19:8 says a person who loves their own soul gets wisdom. Although Eve had knowledge that the forbidden tree was not good for man to eat from, she lacked wisdom. If a person neglects to apply what they know, especially when it can be useful to them, they do not fully understand the meaning of their own knowledge. Wisdom is having knowledge, understanding it, and actually applying it. Adam and Eve were given information far beyond the forbidden tree. They had access to the Tree of Life but ignored it. They could have lived forever, but they were led astray by a desire to have what God had (Gen. 3:5).

One of the first things to learn is to get an understanding of what you have instead of looking at what others have. Eve was led by her natural eyes (v. 6). Look beyond what the eye can see. Is it beneficial to you? Is there a potential for it to cause harm? Is it sustainable? When you love yourself, you will seek the best for yourself—far beyond what the eyes can see.

Love is the foundation for everything God ever did for us. John 3:16 says, "'For God so loved the world that He gave His only begotten Son, that whoever believes in Him should not perish but have everlasting life.'" God put into place salvation because of His love for us, not because we deserve it. Our love for others should display our desire for them to be saved. Our love for ourselves should display our desire to be saved and become all that God has ordained us to be. Love is trusting, following, and obeying God. If we do this, then everything else will follow (Matt. 6:33).

Suggested Readings

Genesis 2:9; 3:17-24; Matthew 26:6-10

While reading Genesis, note the differences and similarities between Adam and Eve with regards to accountability. In Matthew, note the response of the woman in Bethany as her actions were criticized by the disciples.

Accountability

1. Would you say you're a person of accountability? Before you say "yes," are you accountable in all areas of your life? Do you own your actions, responses, and decisions, or do you find reason to blame others for your decisions? Share how you are accountable or unaccountable.

_____

_____

_____

_____

_____

_____

2. Eve must have felt she had no one to turn to when Adam deserted her. Of course, God was right in that He chastised her. It was out of love for her. He knew that Adam and Eve would have to die because of their sin, but that was not what God wanted for them. Instead of Eve looking to God for forgiveness, she began to blame the serpent. Who do you turn to when you make a mistake and why? Do you feel you are accountable to this person?

3. Do you believe God looks for accountability from you in your daily walk? Explain your answer. In what ways do you meet or attempt to meet God's expectations?

_____

_____

_____

_____

_____

_____

_____

_____

_____

_____

_____

4. What are some things you believe you must do to be more accountable in your life? Do you have a plan to get there? If so, write it now.

_____

_____

_____

_____

_____

_____

_____

_____

_____

_____

_____

Adam and Eve had a choice. God told Adam about the differences between the trees in the garden (Gen. 2:16). They made the choice to disobey, but when it came time to stand before God, Adam and Eve abandoned accountability. They were unable to stand in the decision they had made.

The woman in Bethany also had a choice. As Jesus' disciples voiced complaints questioning her motives and ability to make decisions, she stood by her choice without saying a word. Only Jesus spoke in her defense (Matt. 26:10).

Where there is no accountability, there is neglect and failure. Everyone is accountable to someone. It all depends on whether or not we own it. When around parents, bosses, and teachers, we want to put our best feet forward. However, since people do not see God face-to-face, we either tend to slack off or justify our behavior. Just like Adam and Eve, others look for excuses. Nevertheless, the day will come when everyone will be held accountable.

5. Place a √ in front of the statement that shows accountability and an x in front of the one that does not.

☐ After he was removed from the Garden of Eden, Adam worked to provide for his family.

☐ My life is pretty much the way it is because of the environment I was raised in.

☐ I own the choices I make, good or bad.

☐ Eve blamed the serpent for her disobedience.

Looking for ways to get out of a situation is not accountability. Accountability includes owning your mistakes, whatever they may be. Making mistakes is not a weakness, but refusing to own them is. Sometimes it takes courage and strength to accept our own shortcomings. But sometimes that is what it takes to build the kind of character the Lord wants to see in us.

Do not allow others to make you feel bad for what was only a mistake. Admit it, seek forgiveness, and seek God for direction. You are made in the image of God. Condemnation does not come from Him. God loves, forgives, and restores. Do your part and God will do His part.

"... For we shall all stand before the judgment seat of Christ ... So then each of us shall give an account of himself to God"

– Rom. 14:10, 12

Suggested Readings

Genesis 2:15-3; 1 Corinthian 13:11; 2 Corinthians 5:10; Galatians 6:7; 2 Timothy 1:7; James 4:17

Responsibility

To be responsible is probably one of the hardest things to do in life. Everyone wants freedom, and those who are saved through Jesus Christ have freedom. However, this does not mean we can do or say whatever we want. We have a responsibility to represent the Kingdom of God. Why? Because He made us in His image, and once we accept Jesus Christ as Lord and Savior, we are now a part of the Kingdom. We can no longer live as if we are lost. We have a responsibility.

Responsibility is part of duty and purpose. One who is responsible will do their best to carry out what they have been given to do. They will strive to make the right decisions because the outcome supports the purpose. Adam and Eve were told not to eat off the forbidden tree; they were to trust and obey God. At least, this was God's expectation of them. They had a responsibility to protect what had been entrusted to them: the key to life and death. If they had obeyed God, Adam and Eve and all of mankind would have never had to die. They held the power of life in their hands and did not even know it simply because they did not understand it. There was total disregard of their responsibility because they were not willing to ask questions. Was this God's fault? No. They had God in their presence but did not seek to know and understand what had been created around them or what had been given to them.

The sadness of this all is that the same unwilling spirit exists today. Unwilling to learn from God. Unwilling to surrender totally to God. Unwilling to serve God. This underdeveloped spirit wants to appear holy but is missing the presence and power of God because it continues to reject God. It welcomes religion but refuses to surrender self to our Lord and Savior, Jesus Christ. Religion is an option. Jesus requires a relationship.

There were good things hidden within Adam and Eve that they had not yet even begun to tap into. We know this because everything that God made was good. Wasting knowledge, time, gifts, and talents is not being responsible. These things are given to us to make us exalt God and reveal who we really are. When we do better, it reflects our Father in heaven. What if Jesus wasted the anointing that was on His life? Would He have raised the dead, healed the sick, or saved the lost? No! But because He did those things, He behaved responsibly. He did what God sent Him to do. Likewise, we were not made in the image of God just to look good. We were made in His image to do good. This reflects God.

Just as God was responsible for both Adam and Eve, He is responsible for you and me. God has provided everything here on earth that mankind will ever want or need. He has fully met His responsibility by sending His Son, Jesus Christ, to save our souls. But we, too, have a responsibility. It is man's responsibility to seek salvation. This is why God has given us His Word to follow. Since the day of Adam and Eve, who had the Tree of Life in their midst, man has had the opportunity to embrace a right relationship with God. Each person has been given the same opportunity for salvation and access to God. Live your life responsibly. Seek God and His wisdom through Jesus Christ. God loves you and wants the best for you. He has given us the best: His only begotten Son. If we are to truly be responsible human beings, we will give Him our best by becoming all that He made us to be.

1. Did Adam have any responsibility regarding Eve and the fruit of the forbidden tree? If so, what was it according to (2:15-17 and vs. 22-23)? and did he behave responsibly?

_____

_____

_____

_____

_____

_____

_____

_____

_____

_____

2. Why do you think Adam dodged his responsibility? What does the scripture say Adam and his wife did when they heard God walking in the garden (Gen. 3:8)? Why do you think this would be Adam's answer to what became his and his wife's problem?

_____

_____

_____

_____

_____

_____

_____

_____

_____

3. Now that you have seen the results of disobedience due to Adam and Eve, share some characteristics that you have already or plan to incorporate into your relationship with the Lord. Some examples might include trusting God, faithfulness shown toward God, etc.

_____

_____

_____

_____

_____

_____

_____

_____

_____

_____

_____

We can learn a lot from Adam and Eve's mistakes. First, we are to always obey God. If we love Him, we will obey Him. That's the requirement according to what Jesus said (John 14:5). Learn to listen. We are to take inventory of what He said. When we have full access, ask questions for understanding through prayer. Learn to wait on the Lord. Love, trust, and obey Him. And when things get messed up, we will not hide. But we will go to Him, acknowledge our sin, ask for forgiveness, and move forward. Be responsible in your relationship with the Lord. He loves you.

"Teach me Your way, O Lord; I will walk in Your truth. Unite my heart to fear Your name"

– Ps. 86:11

DISCUSSION 2
RELATABLE AND RELEVANT

*E*verything God does is with purpose and according to *His* will. While we live in a society where men and women go back and forth about equality, God blessed both and gave each the same authority. One of the things human beings can learn from God is how God the Father, Son, and Holy Spirit operate as one.

While God the Father and the Holy Spirit were clearly present in Genesis 1, the evidence of Jesus being present wasn't as clear because He was not mentioned by name, but He was there. Jesus' connection as a part of the Trinity was and is relevant, for He is an equal part.

When God the Father, Son, and Holy Spirit speak, there is only one sound. God made two human beings: one man and one woman. He made them equally in His image and in relation to Himself and one another. When we learn to operate in harmony with one another, great things can be accomplished in this world. Acknowledging our Creator and His image in which we were made is key to being who we were meant to be. As women, we are relatable and relevant within the creation of mankind. We must walk in it in the natural and the spiritual. Our Lord and Savior can show us the way by showing us who we are.

Jesus took on flesh and came to show us how to live this life in the flesh and the Spirit. We can look at the ways He operated within the Trinity while walking in a spirit of humility among humanity.

Suggested Readings

Genesis 1:1-4, 26-30; Proverbs 18:22; Luke 1:26-38; John 8:29; 1 Corinthians 13:11

Everything Jesus ever did was good. He was always present with God the Father and the Holy Spirit. When God could not find anyone else to send to save our souls, He sent His Son, Jesus. When Jesus was baptized, God said, "... 'This is My beloved Son, in whom I am well pleased'" (Matt. 3:17). It was obvious that God the Father loved His Son. Jesus never disobeyed God once He took on flesh. Although He became just like any human being, Jesus never sinned; He never strayed away from God.

When God made mankind in His image, He established a relationship with both man and woman. But both man and woman sinned. Did Adam and Eve commit sin because they did not know their identities? What made them yield to the temptation of a serpent when they actually had dominion over it?

Sometimes when a person does not know who he or she is, they can become lost. This did not happen to Jesus. While on earth, He had been walking in His identity since the age of twelve. He knew who He was, so He began walking in it (Luke 2:41-52). Even when His parents, Mary and Joseph, questioned Him, Jesus answered, "... 'Why did you seek Me? Did you not know that I must be about My Father's business?'" (Luke 2:49). Perhaps His mindset was that He must walk, talk, and live as the Son of God. Once the boy Jesus realized who He was, He went to the temple to begin working on His Father's business.

Later in life, Satan attempted to deceive Jesus by questioning Him and tempting Him. This was the way the enemy deceived Adam and Eve. After Jesus had spent forty days and nights fasting in the wilderness, the enemy approached Him, but Jesus did not give in to Satan. Jesus knew who He was, whose He was, and the Word on which He stood. Knowing who you are makes a difference in how you operate and relate to others, including the enemy and even God.

Humans are the only ones made in God's image. We are the only ones with His Spirit and filled with His love. It is mindboggling how those who profess to be atheists can fall in *love*, have a loving family, and deny the very God from which that love came (1 John 4:7-9). Humans are the only beings that God breathed the breath of life into, which positioned man to do great things.

As a person becomes older, they grow out of one stage and into another. Therefore, they should behave differently. The Apostle Paul said, "When I was a child, I spoke as a child, I understood as a child, I thought as a child; but when I became a man, I put away childish things" (1 Cor. 13:11). He understood he had to change.

When God delivered the children of Israel out of Egypt, they had to change. They could not go to a new place, stage, or level being the same way they were in Egypt. At each stage of our lives, roles, rules, boundaries, and trials change. This is why it is so important to remain relatable and relevant in our relationship with the Lord.

Women Are Relevant

We know we are relatable to mankind because woman was made from a rib taken from man. And we were made in the image of God, meaning we are spiritual beings by way of His Spirit—the breath of life. I imagine women are close to God's heart, for He made Eve to give Adam a helpmate, or helper. This was not to diminish woman's importance, responsibility, or position; it was to give Adam what he needed: a woman who could work alongside him, support him, love him, and encourage him. She would be a help to him—a wife.

As women, we are natural at nurturing others whether they are kin to us, friends, or strangers. Some of us have a distinct ability to make others feel at ease. However, there seems to be a thought among some that women are not as relevant. Women are just as relevant as men.

God did not create Eve *just* for Adam. He made her to be a helper relatable to him. However, this was just one of her purposes. When God blessed *them*, He gave Eve the same authority He gave to Adam (Gen. 1:26-30). This demonstrated that she was just as relevant as Adam was. But did woman understand who she was? Did she know of at least one of the blessings God had bestowed upon her? Did Adam's treatment toward Eve inform how she would see herself?

Today, we live in a society that determines the relevancy of women based so much on the outward appearance. It's rare that people look in their eyes to see who's really there. The two and a half years of the pandemic COVID-19 forced us to really see one another because we could only see the eyes of the person. The outward appearance didn't matter so much. We began to see and acknowledge one another.

We, as women, are relevant because the Lord made us that way. We must walk, talk, live, and love ourselves, our husbands, families, friends, and one another as if we are relevant. Our spoken words should make a positive difference in our lives as well as in the lives of others. Our giving should change an outcome for someone and also for ourselves. Our existence should reveal what living looks like in the natural and in the spiritual. We are relatable and relevant. And as women, we are to be everything that our Lord has ordained and expects us to be.

Discussion

1. In what ways are women similar to the Holy Spirit in the Bible?

2. Is it possible for a woman to be a helper and harm another person, or herself, at the same time? If so, explain.

_____

_____

_____

_____

_____

_____

_____

_____

_____

_____

3. Have you ever found yourself being a help or support to others while sabotaging your own joy, peace, and happiness? Explain your answer.

_____

_____

_____

_____

_____

_____

_____

_____

_____

_____

_____

4. What helped you to see that your future, hopes, and dreams are just as important as those that you care about? Explain your answer.

_____

_____

_____

_____

_____

_____

_____

_____

_____

_____

5. What commitment(s) can you make to yourself to live an intentional life as you relate to others, and how are those intentions relevant to you becoming the spiritual person you desire to be?

_____

_____

_____

_____

_____

_____

_____

_____

_____

_____

_____

Never allow the enemy to use you or your gifts, talents, title, position, or ideas for harm. The enemy took the authority Eve had and used it against her. He made her feel like she could be important, but she was already important because she was made in the image of Almighty God. We are to be helpers, not harmers.

What if Adam did not recognize his favor from God? Would this change why Eve was made in the image of God and given the characteristics of a helper? No, it would not. Did Eve's sin change her potential or her gifts within? No, it did not. We were made to be helpers. The Holy Spirit, the third Person of the Trinity, was called the Helper by Jesus Christ. This is the best company we could ever hope to be in.

As helpers, we advance the love of God and His goodness all while moving and becoming in His image. Just because one is made in the image of God does not mean one reflects the image of God. We must learn to reflect His image in our everyday lives. And the only way to do this is to be filled with His Holy Spirit. It is His Spirit reflected that others see.

We are not the Holy Spirit. We have some of His characteristics. Being a helper is just one of them. The Bible talks about those of us who have the first fruits of the Spirit (Rom. 8:23). The Holy Spirit is the very beginning of this process. As we grow, we experience other benefits of being filled with the Holy Spirit. The Bible says, "But the fruit of the Spirit is love, joy, peace, longsuffering, kindness, goodness, faithfulness, gentleness, self-control ..." (Gal. 5:22-23).

Being relatable and relevant is not so much about being on stage front and center, except that it is relevant to the Kingdom of God. Therefore, it is less about the natural side of us and more about who we are spiritually. This is how we are to be helpers—with the intention that all eyes are on the Lord. As the woman in Bethany went in to do something to help Jesus, she never focused on herself. Her focus was always on the Lord.

Agree with God

We must come into agreement with God and submit to His truth even when it hurts. It could not have been easy for Jesus on the cross because He cried out, "... 'My God, My God, why have You forsaken Me?'" (Matt. 27:46) This, more than physical pain, had to strike a nerve with Jesus because, for a moment, He thought the Father had deserted Him. There are things we must go through to get to where God wants us to be. Although He had done nothing wrong, Jesus was punished to death to get us into a right position with God the Father. That is, the very place we were supposed to be. Are you willing to put in the work to get to where you are supposed to be? A good work? Then you must come into agreement with God.

At best, we live a small percentage of who we should be. This, again, is because we live so much more according to the flesh rather than according to the Spirit. Some people try to become spiritual on Saturday or Sunday, depending on what day they go to church. First, we cannot become spiritual. The Holy Spirit is a Person. He must live within us once we have accepted Jesus Christ as our Lord and Savior (Acts 19:5-6). We must agree to allow Christ, through His Spirit, to dwell in us at all times.

We must agree with God that we are made in His image. Before God created man or woman, He said, "Let Us make man in Our image, according to Our likeness ..." (Gen. 1:26). We are meant to be like God the Father, Son, and Holy Spirit. We have God's breath in us. Every breath we take says He's near us. But the flesh takes over and suppresses the spirit in which we were made to operate in, leaving us exhausted yet always looking for more of something to fill that emptiness in which the Spirit of God is to thrive.

How does one move into a place of agreement with God so that he or she can operate as one who is relatable and relevant according to the Lord's will and ways?

He or she must change. The book of Genesis says the earth was without form and void; darkness was on the face of the deep (v. 2). One of the first things recorded that God did was to call forth light (v. 3). That light changed the atmosphere so much that God saw that it was good (v. 4). We have to change, surrender, or do whatever it takes to get into agreement with God.

Read Romans 12:1-2. Change can be a sacrifice, and it can (and sometimes will) hurt.

List some reasons you believe people fear change.

1. _____

2. _____

3. _____

4. _____

5. _____

6. _____

Below are a few reasons why some people are afraid of change. This list is not exhaustive.

- Fear of losing the self they know.
- Fear of being misunderstood by others.
- Fear of losing those they thought were friends, loved ones, or significant others.
- Fear of having to start over.
- Fear of having to deal with hurt.
- Fear of going through it alone.

Change has to take place in order to move into the things God has for us. One way to do this is as the Apostle Paul said to present our bodies a living sacrifice, holy and acceptable to God (Rom. 12:1). This is the reasonable thing to do. It is too late to change once one has passed on. We have to make changes now as we live.

Suggestions to support one in changing their ways:

- Pray. Exalt God. Tell Him who He is to you. Praise Him for who He is. Ask the Lord to make His presence known. Ask for His guidance, discernment, peace, strength, and whatever you think you will need on this journey.
- Surrender to the Lord.
- Change your thinking. When your mind becomes flooded with negative thoughts, start talking or singing to God. Praise God in the midst of the thoughts.
- Resist the enemy and he will flee (James 4:7).

- Resist the ways of the world. Sometimes you have to turn off the TV, radio, news, and hearsay.

- Seek the presence of God every day by submitting to Him and inviting Him into your space. Make time for Him.

- Read your Bible for spiritual growth.

- Learn to deny yourself of things not good for you.

- Make space for "me time" to nurture yourself, reflect, write down your goals, and remember your dreams and revisit them.

- Do something (big or small) to help someone else without expecting anything in return.

We were made to live according to the Spirit of God. We were created to relate to Him and mankind. Agree with God about who He says you are. Regardless of what others might think, as women, we are relatable and relevant. Put in the work and become all you can be. Your light will shine, and God will get the glory.

DISCUSSION 3
BE MINDFUL

*I*n Chapter 3, we discussed one of the main differences between Eve and the woman in Bethany: Their goals were opposite of one another. Eve's goal was to taste the fruit God had commanded her not to eat, and the woman in Bethany's goal was to anoint Jesus before His death. Our goals can determine how focused we are and what we're focused on. There is nothing wrong with being ambitious, but it is wrong to willingly disobey God. Ignoring responsibilities because one's mind is wandering about is not the way of a spiritually mature mind. When we're mindful, our thoughts become more intentional, focused, and assured. We can see that Eve's mind was on Eve, but the woman in Bethany's mind was on Jesus.

In Matthew 26:2, Jesus made a statement that sounded almost like a question. He said, "'You know that after two days is the Passover and the Son of Man will be delivered up to be crucified.'" Although this was a statement, it sounds almost like Jesus was asking His disciples if they remembered His words. However, there is no indication that His disciples remembered or even gave any thought to what Jesus had said. Because they weren't mindful, they did not ask Jesus anything about it. It was as if they ignored what He said.

However, this was not the case. The disciples had not yet learned to control their thoughts and emotions. There were various activities, including the Passover, which would soon take place. It was most likely hard to focus, but Jesus wanted them to be mindful of what

He had told them. They needed to be prepared mentally as much as possible because their lives were about to change in ways they had never known or seen before. They needed to be mindful.

Suggested Readings

Psalm 8:4; Romans 8:1-14; Matthew 26:31-56, 69-75

Discussion

1. Distractions seem to come when important issues need attention. List the ways in which Eve and the woman in Bethany both faced distractions. List how each woman handled her distractions.

_____

_____

_____

_____

_____

_____

_____

2. When we allow our minds to wander, is it possible that we can become a distraction within ourselves? Explain your response. What was Eve's motive for eating from the forbidden tree?

_____

_____

_____

_____

_____

_____

_____

_____

_____

_____

3. God told Adam and Eve what would happen if they ate from the tree. And Eve told the serpent what God said. Yet, because of selfish motives, she was not mindful that the enemy was telling her the exact opposite of what God had said.

Something similar happened between Jesus and Peter in the Garden of Gethsemane. Jesus began to tell His disciples of what was going to happen that night, and Peter began to give Jesus his version of what would happen, even if he (Peter) had to die with Jesus. Have you ever taken over a situation that God did not give to you? If so, what was the outcome, and what lessons did you learn from it?

_____

_____

_____

_____

_____

_____

_____

_____

4. When or where do you think you lost focus? Did you think it was about you, as if God needed you to take care of the situation?

_____

_____

_____

_____

_____

_____

_____

_____

_____

_____

"For to be carnally minded is death, but to be spiritually minded is life and peace"

– Rom. 8:6

5. In your own words, write what it means to be mindful.

_____

_____

_____

_____

_____

_____

_____

_____

_____

_____

_____

6. Write out Romans 8:5-6.

_____

_____

_____

_____

_____

_____

_____

_____

_____

_____

_____

7. Based on the scriptures you have read in Matthew, whose minds were on the things of the flesh? Whose mind was on the things of the Spirit? Explain your answer.

_____

_____

_____

_____

_____

_____

_____

_____

_____

_____

8. How does your meaning of mindfulness relate to Romans 8:5-6? Explain your answer.

_____

_____

_____

_____

_____

_____

_____

_____

_____

_____

_____

9. Do you see why Jesus wanted His disciples to be mindful of what was about to take place? Explain your answer. How does being focused help you to prepare for the future?

_____

_____

_____

_____

_____

_____

_____

_____

_____

_____

10. How can allowing distractions (such as selfish motives) potentially harm the outcome of what God has planned for you?

_____

_____

_____

_____

_____

_____

_____

_____

_____

_____

_____

11. Adam and Eve forfeited the right to live forever when they disobeyed what God said (Gen. 3:22-24). Peter denied Jesus just as Jesus said he would (Matt. 26:75). Write down your plan for staying focused, for being mindful of the things the Lord has told you or showed you. After you are done, read it out loud to the Lord.

_____

_____

_____

_____

_____

_____

_____

_____

_____

_____

_____

Jesus died for our sins and restored a broken relationship so that we can have access to God the Father. He has given us the opportunity to live life and live it more abundantly (John 10:10). We must remain mindful of this. He wants us to remember His Word and what He has done. There are always things going through our minds. The Lord wants us to determine what those things will be. We must learn to focus and intentionally seek the things that will help us to grow spiritually. The Lord is not against your dreams, goals, or plans. After all, He gave them to you. He wants you to include Him in all things related to you. He loves you.

The woman in Bethany did not stop until she had performed what she set out to do. She set her mind and met her goal. Her goal was Jesus. When we allow a desire for the Lord to take first place in our hearts, minds, soul, and body, we will not so easily fall. He has to be first. Everything else will fall into place.

Be mindful of the Lord. He is mindful of you.

"What is man that You are mindful of him, and the son of man that You visit him?"

– Ps. 8:4

DISCUSSION 4
RELIGION BUT NO RELATIONSHIP

We have no real indication that the woman in Bethany was a religious woman, but we know she believed in relationship. She went to Jesus alone with her expensive fragrant oil and poured it on Him. Her actions acknowledged that she believed who He was.

God demonstrated His desire for a relationship with us when He extended love through His Son, Jesus Christ. God gave His only begotten Son, Jesus, to die for our sins. Those who choose to believe will have eternal life. Jesus describes this as knowing the only true God and His Son Jesus, whom the Father sent (John 17:3). Relationship is eternal life. It is forever where the Lord is concerned.

Suggested Readings

Acts 5:1-10; John 3:16, 17:1-3, Matthew 3:14-17, 11:7-11, and 26:13

The woman in Bethany could have gone to Jesus, fallen at His feet, and worshipped Him. And it would have been seen for what it was: an act of worship. There is nothing wrong with that. But she chose to provide a needed service. Someone needed to anoint Jesus, and that is what she did.

Relationships vary depending on the people involved. The Lord is looking for a committed relationship. The woman in Bethany demonstrated a heart for the Lord Jesus. She could have kept back her expensive fragrant oil for herself, but she did what she was led in her heart to do. That was to give it for the use of anointing Jesus. Using the oil the way she did surprised Jesus' disciples, even upsetting some of them.

This was the opposite of what Ananias and his wife Sapphira did in the book of Acts. They thought they had only lied to men when they had actually lied to God to keep part of the money for themselves.

In relationships, we are open about our feelings. Truth and honesty are expected. When Jesus was baptized, God the Father acknowledged Jesus as His Son, sharing that He was pleased with Him. God did not have to acknowledge Jesus. He chose to because of Their relationship. He wanted it to be known this was personal. This was His Son.

When Jesus told His disciples about John the Baptist, He did not speak from secondhand information. He spoke based on His relationship with John the Baptist, who also had a relationship with God the Father. Jesus knew the Father would send John the Baptist before Him. He acknowledged John the Baptist for who he was and what he had done, as he led the way for Jesus. This was a special relationship on different levels.

Relationships are personal and have the ability to grow into beautiful things. This is what happened with the woman in Bethany. Her love for Jesus led Him to demonstrate what He thought about her and her act of kindness. Her work would become known wherever the gospel was preached throughout the world. A relationship had developed.

It was not religion the woman in Bethany demonstrated. It was a commitment. She did not change her mind once she got to Jesus. She did not back out when His disciples began to ridicule and chastise her. She did not allow the fact that Jesus was in the house of a leper keep her from going in. She was after a relationship with her Lord, regardless of the cost.

Discussion

1. Do you consider yourself to be a religious person? Why or why not?

_____

_____

_____

_____

_____

_____

_____

_____

_____

_____

_____

2. In your own words, write what religion means to you.

_____

_____

_____

_____

_____

_____

_____

_____

_____

_____

3. How do you associate with Jesus Christ the Lord? Who is He to you?

_____

_____

_____

_____

_____

_____

_____

_____

_____

_____

4. What role do you occupy in the relationship with Jesus? Who would He say you are to Him? Explain your answer.

_____

_____

_____

_____

_____

_____

_____

_____

_____

_____

5. Does your interaction with others reflect your relationship with the Lord? How?

_____

_____

_____

_____

_____

_____

_____

_____

_____

_____

_____

6. Compare religion and relationship. Which would you describe as activity driven? Which would you say is alive and has the ability to thrive, becoming greater? Explain your answers.

_____

_____

_____

_____

_____

_____

_____

_____

_____

_____

7. How do you recognize the Lord's voice (a sound, prompting, or unction in your spirit) when He speaks to *you*? Have you recognized it is Him and trust that you know it's Him? Explain your answer.

_____

_____

_____

_____

_____

_____

_____

_____

_____

_____

8. Do you depend on others to tell you what the Lord is saying to you in your relationship with Him? Explain your answer.

_____

_____

_____

_____

_____

_____

_____

_____

_____

_____

9. If you depend only on others to tell you what the Lord has to say to you, do you also depend on others to tell you what your spouse, family and friends, want to say to you? Why or why not?

_____

_____

_____

_____

_____

_____

_____

_____

_____

_____

10. If you do not need to rely on anyone to speak to you for your spouse, family, and friends, why would you rely on someone to speak to you on behalf of the Lord? The same way you know your parent's voice is the same way to learn the Lord's voice. You spend time with Him and allow Him to spend time with you. He wants a relationship with you, and He is capable of leading the relationship. Are you willing to participate in a relationship with the Lord starting right now? What could keep you from entering a relationship with the Lord?

_____

_____

_____

_____

_____

_____

_____

_____

_____

Do you believe there is something in your past that would keep the Lord away from you? Why or why not? If so, write it down and give it to the Lord. Repent if needed and accept the Lord's grace. He loves you, and the Bible says there is nothing that can separate you from His love. He wants a relationship with you, but you have to want it too.

_____

_____

_____

_____

_____

_____

_____

_____

_____

"For I am persuaded that neither death nor life, nor angels nor principalities nor powers, nor things present nor things to come, nor height nor depth, nor any other created thing, shall be able to separate us from the love of God which is in Christ Jesus our Lord."

– Rom. 8:38

Build your relationship with Jesus Christ. How? Below are some ways to do this. This is not an exhaustive list, but it's a good place to start.

Building a Relationship with the Lord:

1. Receive the gift of salvation, which is the right to have eternal life with God the Father, the Son, and the Holy Spirit. All is restored by Jesus Christ who died on the cross at Calvary.

2. Confess you are a sinner and want to be saved. You believe in your heart the only way to be saved from an eternity of death is to accept Jesus Christ as your Lord and Savior who died for your sins and whom God raised from the dead (Rom. 10:9-10).

3. Understand salvation is by faith. As your faith grows, so will the evidence of Jesus in your life. Jesus said if we have faith the size of a mustard seed, then we can move mountains (Matt. 17:20).

4. Stay strong through prayer and the reading of God's Word, the Holy Bible. Focus on the Lord and not your circumstances (Isa. 26:3).

5. Meditate on His Word. Remember, as long as you are in relationship with the Lord, no weapon formed against you shall prosper (Isa. 54:17).

6. Learn to speak with the Lord as if talking with a dear friend for whom you have the utmost respect. When you have concerns, tell them to Jesus. He has all the answers. Seek to do His will and He will guide you in the way you should go (Matt. 6:24-34).

7. Speak to the Lord daily, acknowledging Him every morning. Thank Him for the beautiful sunshine and the much-needed rain. Thank Him for He is your covering as you lay down at night and as you go about your business throughout the day (Ps. 121:5-8).

8. Teach your children about the Lord (Ps. 127:3; Isa. 54:13; Matt. 19:13-15).

9. Surrender all that you have to the Lord. Make Him the head of your heart. If you stay with Him, He will stay with you (Matt. 7:24-27).

10. Understand it is your heart He sees. Your body is His dwelling place by way of His Holy Spirit (Rom. 12:1-2; 1 Cor. 6:19-20).

11. Remember He died for you. He will not do anything to hurt you. He loves you and only wants the best for you. Trust Him and obey Him. Obedience is your way of showing your love for Him (John 14:13-18).

"God cherishes relationships with His children. Don't leave Him. He will never leave you."

– Deut. 31:6

DISCUSSION 5
WOMAN

omen are more than curves, hair, and lipstick. We are a necessity. The day God made Eve and took her to Adam was evidence that women were needed. As females, we represent one half of human creation. Being needed means we were made with purpose. Since God made us with purpose, we ought to live with purpose.

There are responsibilities based on the commandment given by Jesus that we should do our best to fulfill in our relationship with the Lord. One day, a lawyer asked Jesus,

"Teacher, which is the great commandment in the law?' Jesus said to him, 'You shall love the Lord your God with all your heart, with all your soul, and with all your mind.' This is the first and the great commandment."

– Matt. 22:36-38

First, we are to love the Lord with all of our hearts and be fully committed to Him. This is the one condition that Jesus gives; it's all or nothing.

We are to love God with all our soul, which is the spiritual birth or beginning of man through God. Genesis 2:7 says, "And the Lord God formed man of the dust of the ground, and breathed into his nostrils the breath of life; and man became a living soul" (KJV). I believe the soul contains who we really are or can become. Because we have been taught to operate in the flesh, we lack the know-how to fully walk in the spirit. Our souls are not connected to anything in this world, which is why we are constantly looking for something to fulfill us. We cannot be fulfilled by material things. They will never be enough. We are spiritual beings and we would be lost if left here to survive.

Jesus said we are to love the Lord God with all our minds. The woman in Bethany was persecuted for the decision she made to use her expensive perfumed oil to anoint Jesus. But based on Jesus' response, she made the right decision. Communing with God mind-to-mind is a spiritual matter. If we grew up and achieved our childhood dreams, it's because we latched on to what God placed inside of us—from our minds to our hearts to reality.

This may seem like a hard task to love the Lord with all our hearts, souls, and minds. However, the Lord would not have required this of us if it was impossible. He knows what is in us and what we are capable of because He made us. We are capable of doing great things, and it begins with love. Love is the foundation. Looking at how God so carefully created the heavens and the earth and afterwards surveyed them to make sure everything was good is a good indication that He made it all, including us, with love. We come from love. God made Adam first, but He made woman of the same love.

We are loved. And it is not because of the way we look. It is not because of the way we're shaped. It is because we come from God. You were intentionally, purposefully, spiritually, and lovingly made by God.

Discussion

1. Do you believe God meant it when He said you, a woman, are to help fill the earth and have control of everything on it? Could He have been talking about you? Explain your answer.

2. Do you think it matters to God whether you are a woman? Why or why not?

_____

_____

_____

_____

_____

_____

_____

_____

_____

_____

_____

3. Do you know filling the earth is about more than giving birth to babies? Women give birth to dreams, ideas, inventions, and so much more. What are you multiplying and filling the earth with?

_____

_____

_____

_____

_____

_____

_____

_____

_____

_____

4. How have you allowed the Lord's unconditional love for you to help you navigate your way through life so far? Is He allowed access to your heart, dreams, and fears? Explain your answers.

_____

_____

_____

_____

_____

_____

_____

_____

_____

_____

We know that God is love because the Bible tells us so in 1 John 4:8 and because He has been present before the beginning (Gen. 1:1). His love represents the foundation of all good things. Too often, our love for the Lord may not be as it should be because our love for ourselves is not as it should be.

5. List some characteristics that you love about yourself that have nothing to do with your physical appearance. List some that others seem to love or like about you.

_____

_____

_____

_____

_____

_____

_____

_____

6. Based on your answers, are you able to see yourself—the real inner you? Do others see the real you? Explain your answers and how they make you feel.

_____

_____

_____

_____

_____

_____

_____

_____

_____

_____

7. Will you give the Lord access to your mind regarding the good and bad thoughts about yourself? Explain your answer.

_____

_____

_____

_____

_____

_____

_____

_____

_____

_____

_____

8. Your soul comes from the Lord, and it is He who makes you alive. Does this make it easier to love Him with the soul that already belongs to Him? Explain your answer.

_____

_____

_____

_____

_____

_____

_____

_____

_____

_____

9. Complete the following statements.
   The Lord wants me to love Him with all of my heart because my heart is...

The Lord wants me to love Him with all of my mind so that my mind is...

_____

_____

_____

_____

_____

_____

_____

_____

_____

_____

The Lord wants me to love Him with all of my soul because my soul is...

DISCUSSION 6
RESTRICTED ACCESS

The Lord had given Adam and Eve access to everything with the exception of one tree in the Garden of Eden. Because the Lord had given them free will to go about on their own, Adam and Eve could do whatever they wanted. However, the Lord commanded them to not eat from the Tree of the Knowledge of Good and Evil (Gen. 2:16-17). We know by now that Adam and Eve ate from the tree; this is how sin started.

Adam and Eve disobeyed the Lord and were restricted from the entire Garden of Eden because in the garden was also the Tree of Life. If they had eaten from the Tree of Life instead of good and evil, man would have been able to live forever. But because of their sin, God restricted their access, never allowing them to enter the Garden of Eden again (Gen. 3:22-24).

It's sad to say, but Adam and Eve misused what they had in their possession. If only they had just taken inventory of what the Lord had given to them. Instead, they followed the serpent, who led them away from a blessing of abundance, and eternal life.

This wasn't much different from the religious men who were after Jesus to kill Him (Matt. 26:3-5). Had they believed Jesus was the Son of God, they would not have been restricted from getting close to Him. But God knew their wicked hearts and how they only pretended to have a relationship with Him. They did not have a relationship with God the Father because they did not have a relationship with His Son, Jesus Christ. They, along with others, were restricted of access.

You may be wondering why some people don't come around you like they used to. Or perhaps you don't get invited or included in social engagements and functions like you used to. Like with Jesus, sometimes God establishes parameters because He has set you aside for His purpose. Some people and social gatherings are nothing more than distractions.

It is a privilege to be considered off-limits because the Lord has set His sights on you and your future. Some plans He has for your life have not been revealed because some things cannot be revealed too soon. Just like with Jesus' anointing, the time has to be just right.

When God has a plan for your life, He will not allow anyone or anything to get in its way. You can allow distractions through your own free will, but you will go where the Father leads if you're obedient to Him just as Jesus was. When God is at work, what you want becomes secondary to what He wants for you. However, He will never force Himself against your will. He has given you the right to make your own decisions, even the ones concerning Him. Each person gets to choose their own way of life or a life through Jesus Christ. Adam and Eve made their choice one day and threw away a life of abundance. I suggest you take inventory of what the Lord has to offer, but it's your choice.

Suggested Readings

Genesis 2-3; 1 Kings 3:5-28; Psalm 105:15; Jeremiah 1:4-10, 29:11; Matthew 10:33

Discussion

1. Have you ever wanted to be a part of a group or club badly but were not allowed in? You did not understand why they did not choose you as wonderful as you are. How do you think the Lord feels when someone refuses to choose Him?

2. Have you ever said "No" to God? Have you ever chosen someone or something over God? If so, who? What? And why? How did it go?

_____

_____

_____

_____

_____

_____

_____

_____

_____

_____

_____

3. When He woke you at 2 a.m. and told you to pray but you went back to sleep, was that a "No"? Were you restricting access to God when He was trying to bless, warn, or protect you?

_____

_____

_____

_____

_____

_____

_____

_____

_____

_____

4. If the Lord gave you access to everything with His permission, what would you ask of Him?

_____

_____

_____

_____

_____

_____

_____

_____

_____

_____

5. What does giving Jesus full access to your life look like?

_____

_____

_____

_____

_____

_____

_____

_____

_____

_____

6. Could He sit and watch your favorite movie with you? Would He be welcomed into all your conversations with family and friends? Why or why not?

_____

_____

_____

_____

_____

_____

_____

_____

_____

_____

7. Could Jesus sit with you at your job? Why or why not?

_____

_____

_____

_____

_____

_____

_____

_____

_____

_____

_____

8. Has the Lord tried to gain access in various ways, but you've never let Him in? Explain.

_____

_____

_____

_____

_____

_____

_____

_____

_____

_____

_____

9. Write all the ways your life has changed since you gave the Lord access to your life. Note all the things He has given you access to since that day.

_____

_____

_____

_____

_____

_____

_____

_____

_____

_____

When the Lord restricts access, it is for our good. When we restrict access to the Lord, we need to check our hearts and our motives.

DISCUSSION 7
VALUE

"For God so loved the world that He gave His only begotten Son, that whoever believes in Him should not perish, but have everlasting life."

– John 3:16

When God the Father sent His Son Jesus to die for mankind, this included men, women, boys, and girls of every race, background, economic status, and pedigree. The Bible says, "Therefore, as through one man's offense *judgment came* to all men, resulting in condemnation, even so through one Man's righteous act *the free gift came* to all men, resulting in justification of life" (Rom. 5:18). Jesus died so that all who believe in Him can have eternal life. God gave His best because He sees value in you.

God valued Adam and Eve and what they contributed to His creation. He also values us today. But our view of what is valuable has to be about more than what we have or can gain. Sometimes this can be hard because of the kind of world we live in. Constant media sources suggest that value is in material things. We constantly see comparisons among houses, cars, bank accounts, and even people. This makes it hard to value the unseen.

Whatever we value in ourselves is usually what we value in others. This is why people of like minds, or those who look similar, tend to associate with one another. But we must be willing to see beyond ourselves and our own perceptions because God loves everyone. The only thing that matters is whether we accept Jesus Christ as our Lord and Savior. This is what truly adds sustaining value to our lives.

Jesus told the story of two brothers. The one who wanted his inheritance from their father took it and went out into the world. It wasn't long before he had spent everything and had nothing to eat because there was also a lack of food in the country. But one day, he decided to go back home and ask his father for forgiveness. His father welcomed him back with hugs and kisses. This is how our Father in heaven views us. When one sins, all she or he has to do is repent and ask God for forgiveness.

He will forgive you because you are important to Him.

Who you are and what you do in life is important. It is not up to others to determine whether who you are or what you do matters. God made you and that makes you important. The Lord did not give us all the same gifts, talents, or ideas. He did not make us all to look the same. But He gave all of us part of His Spirit, the breath of life.

Trust in God that you and what you do in this life are valuable.

When the woman in Bethany faced persecution for anointing Jesus, she did not walk away or separate herself from the group. She continued with what she went there to do. In other words, she did not quit because the disciples disagreed with her actions. Her perfumed oil was valuable, but what she was doing with it was even more valuable.

When Jesus was praying in the Garden of Gethsemane, He did not think He could go through with His assignment. Jesus and the Father had always been one, but something was to take place that could possibly change this, even if for just a moment. Jesus knew that the

Father and sin could never be one, so taking on the sins of the world would mean that He and the Father would become separated. Having this fear of separation was the human side of our Lord and Savior, Jesus Christ. He prayed for the Father to take the cup away from Him. If God chose not to, then Jesus said to let the Father's will be done.

Jesus did not quit. He asked for an out, but He did not quit. He was willing to go through whatever the Father wanted Him to do regardless of the cost. Jesus valued His relationship with the Father more than He valued His own life. If Jesus' sacrifice was what God the Father wanted in order to save our lives, then Jesus was willing to do it. Jesus values all relationships, including the ones with us.

What are you willing to stand for regarding the Kingdom of God? This is a matter of priority, obedience, and trusting God. It is a matter of the heart. You decide what is of value to you. What do you have that God can use? Think about it.

Suggested Readings

John 3:16, 14:27, 15:5; Luke 15:11-32; Matthew 6:19-34, 18:10-14; Romans 5

Discussion

1. In your own words, write what "value" means to you. Write what is most important to you. Explain why you value what you do.

---

2. Describe, in your own words, who you are. This does not include what you do or who you are with regards to other individuals (e.g., mom, daughter, sister, etc.).

_____

_____

_____

_____

_____

_____

_____

_____

_____

_____

_____

3. How is your soul? Are you still connected to the Lord? Why or why not? How do you know?

_____

_____

_____

_____

_____

_____

_____

_____

_____

4. What do you believe Jesus meant when He said, "I am the vine, you are the branches. He who abides in Me, and I in him, bears much fruit; for without Me you can do nothing" (John 15:4-5)?

_____

_____

_____

_____

_____

_____

_____

_____

_____

_____

5. Do you believe the Lord loves those more who seem to have the best material things than those who do not? Why or why not?

_____

_____

_____

_____

_____

_____

_____

_____

_____

_____

6. Do people with lots of money and material things live longer than people without those things? Are they more spiritually connected to God? Explain your answer.

_____

_____

_____

_____

_____

_____

_____

_____

_____

_____

_____

7. If you had a choice, would you prefer lots of money or peace? Explain your answer.

_____

_____

_____

_____

_____

_____

_____

_____

_____

8. What do you believe Jesus is asking you to do when He says not to worry about the earthly things but to seek first above all the Kingdom of God?

_____

_____

_____

_____

_____

_____

_____

_____

_____

_____

9. Do you trust God to take care of you and your family? Do you believe He is willing to? Why or why not?

_____

_____

_____

_____

_____

_____

_____

_____

_____

_____

10. You are the most valuable person (MVP) in the sight of God. Are you content with your life? Write down what your ideal life looks like to you and share it with the Lord. You are important to Him.

_____

_____

_____

_____

_____

_____

_____

_____

_____

_____

11. When you count your blessings, what comes to your mind? Try writing it all down if you can.

_____

_____

_____

_____

_____

_____

_____

_____

_____

_____

Mankind has become good at occupying space within the dimension called the human race. They have bought into a standard set not by God but by mankind ourselves and our perception of what value is. The problem is that the space mankind occupies is more fleshly than spiritual. This is because of sin and how humans have taught one another to view themselves.

This was not God's plan. What is valuable to the Lord is way down deep inside of you. You cannot cover it with makeup, although some try. If you stripped away all of your flesh, it will live. That is who you are—that Spirit-fed soul that God placed in you. It would be terrible to never get to know your true self. When you begin to reach deep inside yourself, you begin to touch God.

When Adam and Eve sinned, God did not remove their souls from them. He simply removed Adam and Eve from the spiritual dimension they once occupied. But God has sent us another window of opportunity through His Son, Jesus Christ. What people forget is that Jesus is not in a grave. He died, rose again, and went back to His rightful place seated in heaven.

He knew the value of what He occupied in the Kingdom. He did not get put out. He came down on His own to save us. We have another chance to live according to the Spirit and not so much of the flesh. It depends on what is important to you. What or who do you value? Whatever you value is what you will seek after.

DISCUSSION 8
A GOOD WORK

What has happened to ground-breaking moments? Where are the earthquakes? Are you willing to go to a place that can cause your soul to tremble? Or do you prefer to remain comfortable?

Groundbreakers and earthquakes make things uncomfortable. The shift moves things out of their usual places. When the woman in Bethany went in and anointed Jesus, His disciples became uncomfortable. How dare she? Jesus, however, was not uncomfortable, for He knew why she was there. When His disciples complained, Jesus asked, "... 'Why do you trouble the woman? For she has done a good work for Me?'" (Matt. 26:10). Although we may not have an assignment such as the woman in Bethany, God still expects good things out of us.

Good works do not necessarily mean things will go exactly the way we want them too. As with Jesus' disciples, some things may cause others to become uncomfortable. They may also make us uncomfortable. We must be willing to work through the process to get to the good part. When God the Father started out with His creation, the Bible says, "The earth was without form, and void; and darkness was on the face of the deep" (Gen. 1:2). This does not sound like a place anyone would want to live, but God saw what it could become. He began to create, and all He created, He saw was good.

We can also see God's creation is good. We experience different seasons throughout the year. We see the birds, trees, and blue skies; we feel the breeze when the wind blows. It is all good. And just as our Father has done good works, He has placed good works within you.

Jesus said to His disciples, "... 'He who believes in Me, the works that I do he will do also; and greater works than these he will do ...'" (John 14:12). The Lord expects you to do good works—even greater than what He has done.

We need the mind of Christ to understand how things work in the Kingdom. Jesus said the woman in Bethany did a good work for Him. He rarely pointed out work done for Him by others. She had carried out an assignment without wavering under pressure. She did not do it for recognition, money, or to get close to Him. She did it to worship Him because she loved Him and wanted to show it.

Jesus acknowledging the work we do is the best compliment any of us could ever receive. Imagine hearing Him say to you, "I am well pleased with what you have done, (your name). You, (your name), have done a good work for Me."

Was it hard to fill your name in the blank? If so, it's likely because you may feel unworthy. Maybe you're thinking about the old you. Be encouraged, for we walk by faith and not by sight. The Lord knows more about you than you know about yourself.

The woman in Bethany was all about Jesus. Can you say that your purpose, regardless of how you serve in your church, community, or organization, is all about Jesus and what He wants? The day will come when we will stand before the Lord and be judged on what we have done here on earth. Will He say, "Well done," or will we look back and see that we have failed?

One day when the sons of God went before Him, Satan went too. God asked him where he had been and Satan answered, "Going back and forth on the earth" (Job 1:6-7). He was looking for those he could destroy. In 1 Peter 5:8, it says we are to be sober and vigilant because the devil goes back and forth looking for anyone he can destroy. Let us not be his agents. Let us work for the Lord.

While Jesus' disciples may not have intentionally opened their mouths to destroy the woman in Bethany, their words were harsh enough to make Jesus question their motives. We should always check our motives before God checks them for us. Let us always strive to do a good work. Let us pray for one another to do good works. The Bible says we are not to grow tired of doing good because, when the time is right, we will reap if we have not given up. Our good works reflect who the Lord is in our lives. Remain steadfast. You will reap a harvest.

Suggested Readings

Genesis 1; 12:2; Psalm 37:4; 75:6-7; Jeremiah 29:11; Matthew 5:16; John 14:9-12; Galatians 6:9-10; Colossians 3:23; James 4:10

Discussion

1. What assignment have you taken on that made you and others uncomfortable? Explain.

_____

_____

_____

_____

_____

_____

_____

_____

_____

2. Since God created us all the same, would it be fair to say judging each other is judging the work of God? Is it possible for me to talk about you and not talk about God? Explain.

_____

_____

_____

_____

_____

_____

_____

_____

_____

_____

3. Why are we opinionated about what God's work should look like in others and ourselves? What gives us the right to judge others and ourselves? Explain.

_____

_____

_____

_____

_____

_____

_____

_____

_____

_____

_____

4. Have you ever had an encounter with God or received an assignment from Him that others did not believe? How did it make you feel? How did you handle the task?

_____

_____

_____

_____

_____

_____

_____

_____

_____

_____

5. What do you think could have happened if God had revealed He was having a woman to anoint Jesus Christ to become king?

_____

_____

_____

_____

_____

_____

_____

_____

_____

_____

_____

6. How do you think the disciples would have responded if a man had anointed Jesus? Do you think they would have questioned, criticized, or ridiculed Him?

_____

_____

_____

_____

_____

_____

_____

_____

_____

_____

7. Can God trust you to do a work for Him even if no one believed you did it? Why or why not?

_____

_____

_____

_____

_____

_____

_____

_____

_____

_____

8. Are our good works about us? Explain your answer.

_____

_____

_____

_____

_____

_____

_____

_____

_____

_____

_____

9. When Jesus hung on the cross all alone for mankind's sins, knowing that the people mocking Him did not believe in Him, how do you think He felt?

_____

_____

_____

_____

_____

_____

_____

_____

_____

_____

10. Would you do the work for God and face persecution if you knew He would say, "You have done a good work for Me" in the end? Why or why not?

_____

_____

_____

_____

_____

_____

_____

_____

_____

_____

God loves you and wants nothing but the best for you. When He is for you, who can be against you? (Rom. 8:31). Ask Him to give you the wisdom, understanding, strength, and courage to do what He would have you do. Thank Him for preparing you for the assignment. Remember, with purpose comes persecution. For if the enemy should use any weapon against you, know the Word of God says it will not prosper (Isa. 54:17).

In everything you do, do it for the glory of God. When His glory shines upon you, no other light can compare. May all your works be pleasing in His sight. And may we all one day hear Him say, "Well done, servant. You have done a good work."

DISCUSSION 9

FAITH

Faith is one of the most powerful tools we have, yet it is probably the least used. People name, claim, and proclaim it, but still nothing happens. Claiming and proclaiming have no power. It is faith that gives our words power.

God has given us everything we will ever need here on this earth and beyond, but faith is our responsibility. Jesus gave His life for our sins. That was His assignment, and He completed the work. If we say we believe it, then we ought to have the faith to walk in it. Studying the Bible for knowledge is fruitless unless we use wisdom and faith to apply it to our lives.

A person can be good at making others feel welcome. They can be a great philanthropist building hospitals for the sick and houses for the homeless, but if they lack the faith to accept Jesus Christ as their Lord and Savior, their soul will be lost.

Faith is not a magic wand to retrieve material things. It is not a magic potion for when one is sick. Faith is one of our greatest resemblances to God. When we operate by faith, we look like Jesus. Faith is not a physical attribute. It is spiritual. Romans 8:14 says, "For as many as are led by the Spirit of God, these are sons of God." "Sons" means mankind and is not exclusive. Those who are led by God walk by faith.

When the Psalmist David wrote "The Lord is my shepherd" in Psalm 23, he wasn't claiming the Lord took him everywhere. David was admitting he also intentionally followed the Lord. The shepherd is one in whom the sheep follow because the sheep trust that the shepherd has her best interest at heart and will keep her safe. The sheep has faith in the shepherd. We have to become as sheep, admitting the Lord knows more about what's best for us than we do for ourselves.

I do not speak of faith as if it is easy to walk in. But the Bible says to whom much is given, much is required. To walk around claiming to believe Jesus has died for our sins, saving us from eternal damnation, yet not living accordingly is a failure to live up to the responsibility we have been called to. We will all have to respond when the time comes.

Building Your Faith

When you learned to walk, you probably stumbled and fell at first, but you got back up and started again. That was because you believed you could. That's faith.

When the woman in Bethany went to Jesus, she did not go seeking anything from Him; she went by faith. God is as close to you as your very own breath because He is your breath (Gen. 2:7). Faith sometimes causes us to surrender what we know to that which we fear we don't know. Yet, it is the only way for us to get to the other side of it. Any fears or doubts the woman in Bethany may have had, she had to get past them.

Approaching Jesus by faith does not mean you have to offer Him an expensive gift or a bag full of money. It just means you have to approach Him believing that He is who He says He is. And that He will do what He said He would do.

Why go to the Lord with an offering? Because this is the beginning of building a relationship by faith. Your heart is the greatest thing you could ever give Him. Once you give Him your heart, you won't have a problem giving anything else.

There are a number of people who claim to believe in the Lord but never build a relationship with Him. It's as if they really don't believe. Jesus said when those people call on Him, He will say He never knew them (Matt. 7:21-23). This is a serious situation. The Lord does not change. So, the one thing you do not want to hear Him tell you is to get away from Him.

Another reason for going with an offering is that Jesus will deliver more than you could ever have given Him. Jesus can fill your heart with so much joy that others will see it as it overflows. I'm sure you've met that person who seems to always have a smile on their face. The woman in Bethany may have been able to put a price on her oil, but she will never be able to put a price on what Jesus did for her. And neither will you.

Faith is our responsibility. We will be held in account for whether we sought a relationship with the Lord. He died on the cross for our sins, and now the rest is up to us to believe and walk in that belief.

I encourage you to read the Word of God. The book of John is one that talks a great deal about Jesus and the work He did on earth. Pray for understanding, discernment, and a desire to get to know Him. Faith can open doors, minds, and relationships.

Suggested Readings

Matthew 15:28; Mark 4:37-41; Luke 12:48; Romans 8:1-16, 10:17-21; Galatians 3:28; 2 Corinthians 5:7; Hebrews 11:6; James 1:6

Discussion

1. Describe faith in your own words. Based on your own experiences, do you have faith? Explain your answer.

_____

_____

_____

_____

_____

_____

_____

_____

_____

2. If you had the faith needed, what might you be able to do that you are not doing now? Or what might you have that you do not have right now?

_____

_____

_____

_____

_____

_____

_____

_____

_____

_____

_____

3. If you lack faith, what might you need to do to change your situation?

_____

_____

_____

_____

_____

_____

_____

_____

_____

_____

_____

4. The Lord wants you to know that if your faith is the size of a mustard seed, it is enough. You do not need to be a Bible scholar, preacher, churchgoer, or teacher. He just wants you to believe in Him and follow Him. Does this help to know He feels this way about you? If so, in what way? What will you do with your big mustard-seed-size faith?

_____

_____

_____

_____

_____

_____

_____

_____

_____

_____

5. The opposite of faith can also be fear. Share how you handle fears whenever they rise up.

_____

_____

_____

_____

_____

_____

_____

_____

_____

_____

6. How has your faith encouraged others (e.g., calling on others to pray for them)? And how does this make you feel?

_____

_____

_____

_____

_____

_____

_____

_____

_____

_____

7. Romans 10:17 says, "So then faith comes by hearing, and hearing by the Word of God." What does this verse mean to you? How do you apply this in your life?

_____

_____

_____

_____

_____

_____

_____

_____

_____

_____

8. Some churches and ministries have statements of faith. Write your own statement of faith based on your current relationship with the Lord or what you would like your relationship to be like.

_____

_____

_____

_____

_____

_____

_____

_____

_____

"... 'I say to you, if you have faith as a mustard seed, you will say to this mountain, "Move from here to there," and it will move; and nothing will be impossible for you."

– Matt. 17:20

DISCUSSION 10
THE ANOINTING — NOTHING WASTED

D o you think the woman in Bethany knew the value of what she had? I believe she did because she used it on Jesus. She could have sold, hoarded, or wasted it. But she chose to use it on the one who had given so much through His presence here on earth.

Jesus knew the value of what He came to do on the earth. One day while in the synagogue, Jesus stood up and began to read from the book of Isaiah. He said,

> "'The Spirit of the Lord is upon Me, because He has anointed Me to preach the gospel to the poor; He has sent Me to heal the brokenhearted, to proclaim liberty to the captives and recovery of sight to the blind, to set at liberty those who are oppressed; to proclaim the acceptable year of the Lord'"

> – Luke 4:18

Jesus was reading the prophecy of Isaiah concerning what Jesus had been anointed to do once He came to earth. He did not waste His anointing.

Matthew 4:23 says, "And Jesus went about all Galilee, teaching in their synagogues, preaching the gospel of the Kingdom, and healing all kinds of sickness and all kinds of disease among the people." He healed Bartimaeus, a blind man who called out to Him for help. Everything that Isaiah prophesied about Jesus, He accomplished. Jesus affirmed the Word, then He went out and performed the Word.

Are you walking in the anointing that the Lord has placed on you? That gift of painting, singing, or making others feel welcome did not come out of thin air. God purposed each one of us with a gift. The anointing on it is from the Lord. If you do not know what your purpose is, ask the Lord. If you know what it is, use it. If it's not as polished as you would like, work on it to get it to where you want it to be. Don't compare yourself to others. Everyone starts out at the same mark: the beginning. The Lord does not intend for you to waste what He has given you.

There is a story that Jesus told His disciples about the man who gave each of his servants talents. Talents were money. The man gave one servant five talents, another servant he gave two, and the third servant he gave one talent. The first two servants took their talents, worked them, and increased them. The third servant, the one with one talent, buried his in the ground.

Sometimes we look over at what someone else has and compare ourselves thinking, *They must be favored by God. They must really be something special that God would bless them with such a gift.* This may sound strange, but it is not so much the gift as it is the Giver.

The Lord does not look over His children and decide to give to one and not the other. Everyone has equal access to all the Lord has created, but it is faith that will determine who will move forward in what the Lord has given them. Some will put in the work and bring it to fruition. They will become what they believed they could be. Others will simply bury theirs. God gives each of us a choice.

I thought perhaps the servant who buried his talent may have felt less than the others because it appeared he received less. However, we must remember it is not the gift but the

Giver that we are to watch because there is always more God can give. God will never run out of gifts, blessings, anointings, or anything else. The men who increased their talents inherited even more.

Everything God placed in and around us is of use. There is nothing He has provided that is to be wasted. This includes people as well. No person should feel overlooked or less than, as if they do not matter. Jonah felt the people in Nineveh weren't worth saving (John 1-4), but who was Jonah to think he could make such a decision for God?

Are not all people created by God? If He made a mistake with one, then He made a mistake with all since everyone comes from one man and one woman. God does not make mistakes; His people are not mistakes. There is something special about each and every one the Lord has given life to. Regardless of your background, your gift and anointing are to be used for God's glory.

Do not waste the life the Lord has given to you. Each day is a gift. Walk in it, enjoy it, and thank God for it. Jesus is the best example of living out a spiritual life in a fleshly body. Jesus wasted nothing. We can also see God's creation is good. We experience different seasons throughout the year. We see the birds, trees, and blue skies; we feel the breeze when the wind blows. It is all good. And just as our Father has done good works, He has placed good works within you.

Jesus said to His disciples, "... 'He who believes in Me, the works that I do he will do also; and greater works than these he will do ...'" (John 14:12). The Lord expects you to do good works—even greater than what He has done.

We need the mind of Christ to understand how things work in the Kingdom. Jesus said the woman in Bethany did a good work for Him. He rarely pointed out work done for Him by others. She had carried out an assignment without wavering under pressure. She did not do it for recognition, money, or to get close to Him. She did it to worship Him because she loved Him and wanted to show it.

Jesus acknowledging the work we do is the best compliment any of us could ever receive. Imagine hearing Him say to you, "I am well pleased with what you have done, (your name). You, (your name), have done a good work for Me."

Was it hard to fill your name in the blank? If so, it's likely because you may feel unworthy. Maybe you're thinking about the old you. Be encouraged, for we walk by faith and not by sight. The Lord knows more about you than you know about yourself.

The woman in Bethany was all about Jesus. Can you say that your purpose, regardless of how you serve in your church, community, or organization, is all about Jesus and what He wants? The day will come when we will stand before the Lord and be judged on what we have done here on earth. Will He say, "Well done," or will we look back and see that we have failed?

One day when the sons of God went before Him, Satan went too. God asked him where he had been and Satan answered, "Going back and forth on the earth" (Job 1:6-7). He was looking for those he could destroy. In 1 Peter 5:8, it says we are to be sober and vigilant because the devil goes back and forth looking for anyone he can destroy. Let us not be his agents. Let us work for the Lord.

While Jesus' disciples may not have intentionally opened their mouths to destroy the woman in Bethany, their words were harsh enough to make Jesus question their motives. We should always check our motives before God checks them for us. Let us always strive to do a good work. Let us pray for one another to do good works. The Bible says we are not to grow tired of doing good because, when the time is right, we will reap if we have not given up. Our good works reflect who the Lord is in our lives. Remain steadfast. You will reap a harvest.

Suggested Readings

2 Kings 13:20-21; Proverbs 22:29; Matthew 25:14-30; Mark 10:46-52; Luke 4:18-19; Romans 6:23; 1 Corinthians 12:5-6; Ephesians 2:10; 1 Timothy 1:15; James 1:17-25

Discussion

1. How often do you use the beautiful gift God gave you to shine for men to see your good works and glorify your Father in heaven? Do you know that is what your gift is for? Explain your answer.

_____

_____

_____

_____

_____

_____

_____

_____

2. In what ways do you strengthen or improve your gifts or talents? If you do nothing to strengthen or improve what you have, why not?

_____

_____

_____

_____

_____

_____

_____

_____

_____

_____

_____

3. Do you feel the need to impress others? Why or why not? If so, does that make the gift about you and not God?

_____

_____

_____

_____

_____

_____

_____

_____

_____

_____

4. What are some lessons learned that you can share with others about using or not using your gifts/talents from the Lord?

_____

_____

_____

_____

_____

_____

_____

_____

_____

_____

_____

5. Who or what would you be if the Lord removed His gift(s) from you?

_____

_____

_____

_____

_____

_____

_____

_____

_____

_____

_____

6. The Bible says, "For the wages of sin is death, but the gift of God is eternal life in Christ Jesus our Lord" (Rom. 6:23). Even if you can't sing, dance, or do anything considered a talent, you have received the greatest gift of all: salvation. What will you do with this knowledge?

_____

_____

_____

_____

_____

_____

_____

_____

_____

_____

_____

7. Jesus was anointed to do great things, and He wasted none of it. What can you share with others about what His life has done for your life?

_____

_____

_____

_____

_____

_____

_____

_____

_____

_____

_____

8. If years have passed by and you never really used your gift, it is not too late. Be encouraged knowing the Lord gave it to you. That makes it good because His blessings can never die. Write down your plan to start using your gift and walking in your anointing.

_____

_____

_____

_____

_____

_____

_____

_____

_____

_____

9. Would God be pleased with how you use your gifts? Why or why not?

_____

_____

_____

_____

_____

_____

_____

_____

_____

_____

10. If you receive all the praises from man, would the Lord say, "You have done a good work"? Explain your answer.

_____

_____

_____

_____

_____

_____

_____

_____

_____

_____

_____

CLOSING THOUGHTS

Is it possible that the disciples found fault because the woman in Bethany was in possession of an expensive bottle of oil? Of course it is possible. Does it matter? No, it does not. What matters is that Jesus refused to cater to the traditions of man, including the treatment of women.

God the Father asked the first woman, Eve, "What is this you have done?" (Gen. 3:13). The question alone is intimidating without factoring that it came from God. Sin had been committed. While it may have looked like God had deserted Eve and banished women forever, He had a plan. Even as He confronted and admonished her, God was planning to take back what the enemy had taken from Eve on that day.

As women continued to face criticism, unfair treatment, and sometimes disgraceful and demeaning comments portrayed as respect, God had a plan. Not only would He restore woman to her rightful place, but He would use her in one of the most incomprehensible spaces to do what was perceived as a man's job. God would use a woman to anoint Jesus Christ.

The woman in Bethany did not seek this assignment, but it was bestowed upon her. Her simple desire to worship Jesus was used to honor and promote Him, and it also promoted her. She did a good work, and Jesus praised her by saying, "… 'For she has done a good work for Me'" (Matt. 26:10).

"Let your light so shine before men, that they may see your good works and glorify your Father in heaven."

– Matt. 5:16

ABOUT THE AUTHOR

Jackie is a mom and a minister. She is a servant of the Most High God, and the founder of Women of Galilee… following Jesus. Teaching the Word of God is her greatest passion. She says, "There is one thing that I know for sure: I am nothing without the Lord." Jackie resides in North Carolina.

ACKNOWLEDGMENTS

Thank you Ms. Kathryn Wilson for always encouraging me to go after God, and to do His will.

I would like to thank Abbey McLaughlin, Copy Editor, for your support and professionalism.

Thank you to the editors of Speak Write Play, LLC.

I would like to thank my daughter, Raini, for helping to stage the items for the book cover and getting a perfect shot with the camera. Your support means more than you will ever know.

Thank you to the readers. I pray "A Good Work" will assist you on your journey, into your destiny.

God is good all the time. And all the time, God is good. Amen.

Min. Jackie

Made in the USA
Columbia, SC
05 May 2024